IF LIFE IS A PIECE OF CAKE
WHY AM I STILL HUNGRY?

DOUG FIELDS

HARVEST HOUSE PUBLISHERS, INC.
Eugene, Oregon 97402

Scriptures quoted from *The Everyday Bible*, New Century Version.
Copyright © 1987 by Worthy Publishing, Ft. Worth, Texas 76137.
Used by permission.

Illustrations by Sandy Silverthorne

**IF LIFE IS A PIECE OF CAKE—
WHY AM I STILL HUNGRY?**

Copyright © 1989 by Harvest House Publishers, Inc.
Eugene, Oregon 97402

Library of Congress Cataloging-in-Publication Data

Fields, Doug, 1962–
    If life is a piece of cake—why am I still hungry?

    Summary: Discusses a variety of problems faced by teenagers and suggests ways of dealing with them from Christian perspective.
    1. Teenagers—Prayer-books and devotions—English.
[Prayer books and devotions.   2. Conduct of life.
3. Christian life]   I. Title.
BV4850.F54   1989   248.8'3   88-34759
ISBN 0-89081-718-9

Printed in the United States of America.

Dedicated to:

Tim Timmons, my friend, my pastor, and my boss; a man who has taught me how to think about impact and how to communicate grace.

Special thanks to:

Cathy, my wife, who was my encouragement, my editor, my sounding board for ideas, and my biggest supporter during the writing of this book.

And the students from South Coast Community Church, who have opened and shared their lives not just as students, but as friends whom I have come to love.

More books by
Doug Fields

How Not To Be A Goon

Creative Dating

More Creative Dating

Creative Times With Friends

Creative Times With God

Creative Romance

Contents

Introduction

During the years I was growing up in church, I never really understood Christianity. I thought that once you made a commitment to Christ, you were required to act perfectly. And if you couldn't act perfectly, you should feel guilty. Therefore, I lived a very guilt-ridden life. I was told that a Christian shouldn't have problems. The Christian life was supposed to be a piece of cake. But as hard as I tried to be a perfect Christian, I still had problems. And since my life wasn't a piece of cake, I wanted to give up and bail out on this perfection trip called Christianity.

It was at my lowest point of desperation that I discovered that it was okay to have problems—even as a Christian. I was relieved to learn that failure, struggles, and hurt were a part of the Christian life. I also began to understand that Christianity is a process, not an overnight accomplishment. I finally felt normal. I decided to give this kind of Christianity a try.

Maybe you also have been discouraged about the problems you have faced as a Christian. That's why I wrote this book—to give you hope. These pages are filled with the problems that many of us deal with on a regular basis. And I've included lots of stories of real people who have shared their struggles with me.

As I prayed about this book, three major thoughts were in my mind. First, I want you to feel normal, that you are not alone in your problems. It's okay to have them and still be a Christian. God understands and His love continues. Second, I want you to be healed as you identify your problems and discover ways to conquer them. God also wants to be a part of your healing process. Third, I want you to be challenged to grow and mature into a stronger man or woman of God. God wants to know you in a more intimate and personal way.

If you've been told that life is a piece of cake, you've been lied to. And if you heard that Christianity was going to be a piece of cake, you were badly misinformed. If you believe either of these untruths, you're going to be hungry and disappointed. But by understanding that failing is a part of living, and that God desires maturity and not perfection, you are on your way to living your life on purpose.

Your partner in problems,
Doug Fields
Newport Beach, California

What would your sign say?

1
IT ONLY STOPS HURTING WHEN IT'S HEALED

This book is filled with the true stories of real people with real problems. For example, Stephanie is 18 years old and weighs 300 pounds. Her huge body is marred by 28 tattoos, half of which, she boasts, are the names of different men. Stephanie hurts badly, and she needs help. But she is unwilling to admit her problems. I desperately want her to know that God is in the healing business, and that His healing is available to her.

You may be thinking that your problem isn't that bad. But this book talks about all types of problems—some of them considered biggies and many others that everybody seems to have. The hardest person to share God's healing with is the person who is unable to admit that he or she is having problems.

You must understand that problems don't happen overnight. You aren't perfect when you go to bed, and then wake up with an eating disorder, a cheating problem, or a bad relationship with your parents.

> *You must understand that problems don't happen overnight.*

Your problems are the result of different flaws in your development. These flaws may be the result of negative feelings and experiences in your past. For example, you may have felt rejected by the significant people in your life, you may have battled with failure, or you may have suffered the constant fear of trying to please others. Any experiences like these in your past can produce problems in the present.

There are five truths to be understood before you begin this book. First, all of us have problems; you are not alone in your pain. Second, there is hope for you in your problems. Third, you are the only one who can make the decision to get help; nobody can do it for you. Fourth, if you don't work on your problems, they will continue to destroy you. And fifth, God wants to be actively involved in your healing process.

As you read through this book, my hope is that you will find and experience God's grace and hope for your problem, no matter how small or large it may be. As you come to understand your need for help in an area of your life, apply this biblical method of healing:

1. *Admit your suffering*: "I have a problem, I want to change, and I need help."

2. *Understand that healing takes time*: "I realize that I'm going to have problems, struggles, and tough times. Healing is a process, not an overnight achievement. I will persevere."

3. *Analyze your feelings*: "I will learn more about myself and how to deal with my feelings during this healing process. I realize that, as I persevere through this problem, I will mature. I will encounter insights and experiences that will build my character and make me a better person."

4. *Anchor your faith in God*: "I understand that there is light at the end of the tunnel. My faith and hope are anchored in God's grace on which I now stand (Romans 5:2; 8:18-27). It is because of God's grace that I can persevere through my suffering and build character." You are not alone in your problems. I pray that you will come to understand that I'm not okay and you're not okay—and that's okay! You're normal, and God wants to be actively involved in helping you become complete and mature in your relationship with Him.

Something to think about:

"And we also have joy with our troubles because we know that these troubles produce patience. And patience produces character, and character produces hope. And this hope will never disappoint us, because God has poured out his love to fill our hearts. God gave us His love through the Holy Spirit, whom God has given to us" (Romans 5:3-5); "We have sufferings now. But the sufferings we have now are nothing compared to the great glory that will be given to us....Everything God made would be set free from ruin. There was hope that everything God made would have the freedom and glory that belong to God's children" (Romans 8:18,21).

MY PERSONAL THOUGHTS AND ACTION STEPS:

STICKS & STONES ARE NOTHING COMPARED TO WORDS

You have probably heard the saying, "Sticks and stones will break my bones, but words will never hurt me." It's a lie. Words are very powerful, especially when directed at others!

Recently, I was with three guys from my youth group, and it seemed like every sentence they spoke contained something like:

"What a jerk!"

"Don't be such an idiot."

"You're so lame."

"Don't be so stupid."

And these guys were best friends!

This kind of negative input happens at home and at school. We hear people saying:

"Sit down and shut up!"

"Leave me alone!"

"Can't you do anything right?"

"Is that your face or did your neck throw up?"

People are dying to hear positive words.

"Why didn't you get your report in on time?"

Think about your language for a minute. What kind of words come out of your mouth? It's important to understand that people are dying to hear positive words. We all crave and need positive, verbal affirmation. The truth is that we have the ability to change lives for the better or destroy them with our words. Each of us holds the key to tremendous power in the words we use every day.

When you constantly feed others negative input, they'll begin to believe it. If you repeatedly tell people that they're ugly, they'll probably begin to feel and act ugly. People have a way of living out the negative words they hear. This is tragic, but the opposite dimension is also true. We can affect others in positive ways by using good words about people:

"You look great today!"

"You really did an outstanding job on that project."

"It's been great talking with you."

"I thought what you said in class helped me understand better."

Compliments like these make people feel good about themselves, and they begin to think, "Somebody noticed something good about me!" Positive words make us feel warm inside, while negative words

"Somebody noticed something good about me!"

freeze our insides with an uncomfortable, painful feeling. Affirmation and encouragement of someone's abilities build his confidence. People will respond to their greatest potential when they feel good about themselves. It's amazing how lives can be changed by simple, sincere, positive words.

There are several reasons why we fail to affirm others. One of the biggest is our low self-image. We're afraid that if we build up someone with positive words, we will look bad by comparison. And we don't want others to look better than we do. These selfish attitudes keep us from loving others and making them look good.

The Bible tells us, "Love each other like brothers and sisters. Give your brothers and sisters more honor than you want for yourselves" (Romans 12:10). Our challenge is to actively search for positive qualities and features in others that we can verbally affirm. What a compliment it would be for you to be known around your school or church as the person who makes others feel special about themselves. Affirming people can be one of the most positive habits in your life. By constantly searching for positive qualities and affirming them in others, you will have a tremendous ministry. Your positive words will reflect the warmth and radiance of God's love. Pray that God will use your affirming words to turn others to the source of everything good and positive—God Himself.

Something to think about:

"Careless words stab like a sword. But wise words bring healing" (Proverbs 12:18).

MY PERSONAL THOUGHTS AND ACTION STEPS:	_____

3

IT'S EASIER TO SPELL ANOREXIA & BULIMIA THAN TO FACE THEM

As a sophomore, Tina's world began to crumble. Life at home was awful, she didn't feel good about her appearance, and she felt isolated from her friends. Nothing seemed right. Tina's guilt about her unhappy life submerged her in depression and she stopped eating—not because she wanted to be thinner, but because she was so depressed. Some of her Christian friends pointed condemning fingers at her, saying that if she was more mature in her faith she wouldn't have an eating problem. She began to believe the lie that Christians aren't supposed to have any problems like anorexia. Her guilt and depression worsened.

Her weight quickly dropped to a fragile 75 pounds. With Tina's calves only the size my wrists, her parents panicked and began forcing her to eat. But her stomach couldn't handle the radical change and it rejected the food. Tina's bulimia wasn't typical either,

> **She began to believe the lie that Christians aren't supposed to have any problems.**

because her vomiting was voluntary, not self-induced. Through all this her feelings were the same. She felt guilty, angry at herself and God, and she hated life almost as much as she hated throwing up. The thought of taking her own life consumed her. She felt out of control and she didn't know where to turn.

19

One Tuesday night as Tina's support group shared prayer requests, she broke into tears. She fought with herself over telling the group her problem, but after several minutes of uncontrollable sobbing, she told the truth to a small group of girls. Tina's friends quickly bonded to her pain. To Tina's surprise, another girl in the group confessed that she had been forcing herself to throw up for over a year. She said she had cried herself to sleep many times over the guilt and pain of being unable to control her life.

Thousands of people have eating problems. They need help, but they are afraid to share their problems—even though it's a common struggle. If you have an eating problem, there are recovery steps that you must work through to find healing. The first step is to admit that you have a problem. Since eating disorders are multi-dimensional, there isn't one solution that works for everyone. Though you are experiencing much pain and confusion, it's important to understand that you're not alone in your problem. People are being healed every day as a result of admitting their problems and seeking help. There is hope. Confessing your problem is your first step.

Something to think about:

"There is no God like you. You forgive people who are guilty of sin. You don't look at the sins of your people who are left alive. You, Lord, will not stay angry forever. You enjoy being kind. Lord, you will have mercy on us again. You will conquer our sins. You will throw away all our sins into the deepest sea" (Micah 7:18-19).

MY PERSONAL THOUGHTS AND ACTION STEPS:

_____

_____

_____

_____

_____

_____

_____

_____

_____

_____

_____

_____

_____

_____

_____

21

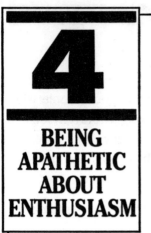

4

BEING APATHETIC ABOUT ENTHUSIASM

Recently, I had a telephone conversation with a guy in our youth group which went something like this:

"Hi, Kevin, this is Doug."

"Hi."

"What are you doing?"

"Nothing."

" 'Nothing'? What do you mean, 'nothing'?"

"I'm not doing nothing."

"You've got to be doing something. Aren't you standing, eating, breathing, thinking, doodling, dreaming, or burping?"

"No, I'm just sitting here watching MTV. It's no big deal. Basically, I'm bored and I don't want to do nothing."

This wasn't an unusual conversation. "Nothing" seems to be a major activity among teenagers. It's frightening to think that so many people do nothing and slowly become apathetic in their lifestyles.

> *"Nothing" seems to be a major activity among teenagers.*

One teacher was so fed up with his lazy students that he wrote the word *apathy* in huge letters on the chalkboard. One student in class asked another, "Do you know what that word means?"

The response was perfect: "Who cares? It's probably just another spelling word."

Apathy means to be without feelings and concern. I

believe the problem of apathy can be counteracted with an opposite extreme: enthusiasm. People with the gift of enthusiasm are rare. I see more students who are depressed, lonely, and trying to hide than those who are bubbling with enthusiasm. But it's tough to be apathetic when your life is filled with enthusiasm. There's an unusual magic about people who are enthusiastic. I love being around enthusiastic people because of their positive outlook on life. They make me feel enthusiastic; it's contagious.

Imagine that we wore neon signs above our heads that flashed descriptive sentences about our attitudes. An enthu- siastic person's sign might flash: "I love life"; "Isn't it great to be

Enthusiasm can make a difference in our lives.

alive?"; or "Life is a blast." But an apathetic person's sign would probably read: "Oh well, I guess it's another day"; "There is nothing to do"; or "I don't care." Which person do you relate to—enthusiastic or apathetic? What would your sign say?

Enthusiasm can make a difference in our lives. It's a powerful force in life which can motivate us, help us reach goals, assist us in selling ideas, enhance our first impressions on people, change attitudes around us, build confidence, relieve fears, boost schoolwork and athletics, improve our appreciation for life, and bring us closer to God.

Try starting each day with an enthusiastic outlook on living. Recite these words, based on Psalm 118:24, as you struggle to get out of bed: "This is the day the Lord has made. I will rejoice and be glad in it." If you place these

23 ■

words in your heart, you'll have a positive expectation for a great day. Then end each day thanking God for the day you have been given, and pray that you might wake tomorrow with an enthusiasm for life and an excitement for the God who created you.

The word *enthusiasm* comes from the Greek words *en theos*, which actually mean "in God." God is the source of energy, vitality, power, and enthusiasm for those who have come into a relationship with Him. There's no better way to find enthusiasm in life than by plugging into the Creator of life. You'll find that apathy can't survive the enthusiasm that is available through God.

Something to think about:

"Enjoy serving the Lord. And he will give you what you want" (Psalm 37:4); "All things were made through him. Nothing was made without him" (John 1:3).

MY PERSONAL THOUGHTS AND ACTION STEPS:	_____
	_____
	_____
	_____

_____

_____

_____

_____

_____

_____

_____

_____

_____

_____

_____

_____

5

IS IT YOUR AUNT, A PRAYER, OR A FREE GIFT?

As a boy growing up in church, I heard the word *grace* a lot. I didn't know what grace was. I just thought the minister was talking about my aunt in Florida whose name was Grace. After I was corrected I changed my definition. Grace was then the prayer we said before dinner. Once again I was corrected. Somebody told me that grace was "undeserved favor." I understood when Grace was my aunt and when grace was a prayer before meals. But what is undeserved favor?

Grace is a gift from God which we don't deserve, but which we receive anyway because He chooses to give it to us. This gift is His unconditional love. God's love is not based on what we do, but on who we are—His creation. There are no strings attached to His gift. I tried to explain this concept one Sunday morning to my youth group by inviting a visitor to come forward and receive a 20-dollar bill as a gift.

> *God's love is not based on what we do.*

She took it, and then tried to give it back. She didn't deserve it and she hadn't earned it, but I wouldn't take it back. My gift to her was only for the sake of illustration. But God's gift to us is an expression of His love. We don't understand it and we don't deserve it, but He gives it anyway.

God gives His grace in loving forgiveness to anyone

who chooses to give his or her life to Him. To the person who is not a Christian, grace is only a word. God loves the unbeliever, but His grace can only be received by those who have accepted a loving relationship with Him through Jesus Christ.

As Christians, we can respond to God's generosity in one of two ways. One way is through arrogant disobeience. This attitude says, "Since God will forgive me anyway, I'm going to blow off Christianity for now, live a lifestyle of sin, and then get back in touch with God when I'm on my deathbed. If grace is available to sinners, what's the point of me trying to work hard in my faith?" Some people call this response "cheap grace," mocking and misusing a precious gift.

The other option is to respond to grace with thankful obedience. This is an attitude that says to God, "I don't understand why You love me enough to give me grace, but I'm thankful and I'm going to show You my appreciation by serving You." Have you received grace from God? Is your life a living response of thankfulness for His generous, unconditional love?

Something to think about:

"So what should we do? Should we sin because we are under grace and not under law? No! Surely you know that when you give yourselves like slaves to obey someone, then you are really slaves of that person. The person you obey is your master. You can follow sin, or obey God. Sin brings spiritual death. But obeying God makes you right with him" (Romans 6:15-16).

MY PERSONAL THOUGHTS AND ACTION STEPS:

6

IT'S A BEAUTIFUL COVER, BUT THE BOOK IS A MESS

After talking with Lindy over a bowl of frozen yogurt, I had to race back to my computer so I could write down her story. Lindy is a perfect example of how easily we can be fooled into believing that people are something they're really not.

Lindy is a junior in high school and the captain of her cheerleading squad. After spending five minutes with Lindy, you'd think she has it all together. On the outside she's pretty, talented, popular, and has lots of friends. But on the inside Lindy is dying. She told me that she doesn't get along with her parents, that she has no boyfriend, and that she's angry with life. Lindy admitted that she's made some stupid decisions which are going to affect her in the long run, and that she's flaking on her present commitments.

It's interesting how we view people as having it all together when they're really falling apart. This is how we look at famous musicians, professional athletes, and movie stars. We'd

All people are basically the same.

give anything to see them, touch them, and talk to them. They appear supernatural, but in reality they're just like you and me. They have real problems—drug addiction, broken marriages, temper tantrums, financial battles, eating disorders, deaths in the family. When we see them on TV, we perceive them as perfect. We think that if there are problems in their lives, they are usually solved before the show is over.

Who's at fault for this misperception? Is it ours for placing unrealistic expectations on outwardly together people, only to be let down? Is it theirs for being such "hot shots" in public and not letting us see their real lives? Or do we just forget that all people are basically the same. They may come in different sizes and shapes, live at different financial levels, and think, play, and speak differently. But no matter how together they may look on the outside, inside everybody is just like you and me— often un-together and in need of love and care.

People misinterpret Lindy in much the same way we misinterpret our heroes of stage, screen, and stadium. She's a perfect example of the old saying, "You can't judge a book by its cover." You may not feel very together on the inside, but be encouraged: in God's eyes, each one of us is a bestseller.

Something to think about:

"Do not think that you are better than you are. You must see yourself as you really are. Decide what you are by the amount of faith God has given you" (Romans 12:3).

MY PERSONAL THOUGHTS AND ACTION STEPS:	_____

_____

_____

_____

_____

_____

_____

_____

_____

_____

_____

_____

_____

_____

_____

7

DO THE CROWDS HAVE YOU CAUGHT IN THE MIDDLE?

Are you ever caught in the middle when trying to make the right decision? For example, let's say you're a Christian, but you run with the popular crowd. Do you have a hard time deciding whether you should continue to hang out with the popular crowd (where you compromise your faith) or with the Christian crowd? You feel better with the popular crowd, especially when you pretend to share things in common with them. You feel comfortable even though there's pressure to do what they do, drink when they drink, talk the way they talk, and think like they think. The more you conform, the more secure you feel in the crowd.

But when you hang around the Christian crowd, they seem so...weird. That may sound mean, but it's true. To the popular crowd, Christians *are* weird. They have their own little cliques. They carry huge Bibles

To the popular crowd, Christians are weird.

to class and debate against evolution loudly. The popular crowd won't go to church because they think Christians are geeks. And when you attend church, it seems like the Christians don't accept you. They may be intimidated by you and your allegiance to the popular crowd. They think you don't care about them, so they question your presence at church by staying away from you.

Finding acceptance in both crowds can be frustrating. Your popular, party crowd doesn't call you because you act a little churchy, and the Christian crowd doesn't accept you because you act a little worldly.

Do you ever get caught like this? You may wonder if God wants you to be a loner on campus, since you don't feel comfortable in either crowd. It's tough to leave the popular crowd because, no matter how spiritual you may become, you still feel a need for their acceptance.

I believe you can have the best of both crowds. I believe you can fit into the Christian crowd and also have an effective ministry with the popular crowd. But it can't happen until you quit playing in the middle. You need to make the Christian crowd your home base. The Christian crowd is going to help move you toward maturity in your faith. As you're moving and growing with the Christian crowd, you can begin to reach the other crowd for Christ. Your acceptance with the popular crowd will help you bridge the gap between the two. You may be able to bring

> *You need to make the Christian crowd your home base.*

people from the popular crowd to church as a result of your previous relationship. By bringing them one at a time, you will find them more open to the Christian message because they won't feel the need to play the popular role when their friends are not around.

If you are caught in the middle, God may be urging you to take a stand with your Christian brothers and sisters, and become a light in the midst of the darkness you came from.

Something to think about:

"You are the light that gives light to the world. A city that is built on a hill cannot be hidden. And people don't hide a light under a bowl. They put the light on a lampstand. Then the light shines for all the people in the house. In the same way, you should be a light for other people. Live so that they will see the good things you do. Live so that they will praise your Father in heaven" (Matthew 5:14-16).

MY PERSONAL THOUGHTS AND ACTION STEPS:

_____

_____

_____

_____

_____

_____

_____

_____

_____

_____

_____

_____

_____

8

WHO AM I CHEATING BY CHEATING?

Rob and Jackie, two friends from the high school group, were at our house talking about the first two weeks of school. The issue of cheating came up. Rob said he didn't know one person in his school that wouldn't cheat if he or she had the chance. Jackie said that some girls on her cheerleading squad had been suspended for swiping a teacher's answer sheet. The longer we talked, the more convinced we became that cheating is almost universal—it seemed like everyone does it. Even the brainy students, who don't need to cheat, contribute to the problem by allowing others to copy.

Rob explained that the humiliation of being caught two years earlier keeps him from cheating. "I'll never cheat again; it isn't worth the embarrassment."

"I feel that cheating at school is no different than lying or stealing," Jackie added. "I know several Christians who cheat." We agreed that cheating isn't only a non-Christian issue.

> *Cheating is no different than lying or stealing.*

We talked about the motivating forces that prevent people from cheating. The fact that cheating is wrong keeps very few from the act. It's like speeding. Driving over the speed limit is wrong, but we all do it. We came up with three reasons why we shouldn't cheat:

35

1. *Cheating breeds apathy*: Apathy is the attitude that says, "I don't care." Knowing you can cheat successfully lowers your desire to study and the challenge to succeed in school. Why study and risk failure when you can cheat and get the right answers? There are a lot of other things you can do which are more fun than studying, especially when you know you don't need to.

2. *Cheating makes others feel uncomfortable*: Cheating puts others on the spot. Usually the person who studies doesn't want to cheat, but he does because of the pressure. Also, there are people in your class that you are trying to bring to church and reach for Christ. But when you cheat, you lose their respect. And when you talk to them about God, you smell like a hypocrite.

3. *Cheating steals the gift of education*: When we cheat, we take for granted the gift of education. If we could look back through our family histories we would find people who weren't allowed to get an education. We are a privileged generation and don't realize it. When I cheated in school, I threw away some needed pieces from the puzzle of my complete education. I didn't realize that someday I would need that material and want to know it. I'm presently working hard to read things that I blew off in high school. I'm embarrassed about this.The temptation to cheat is great. The pressure for grades is demanding. Making your parents happy is important. But when you cheat, you miss out. If cheating is a problem for you, you need to rethink your reasons for cheating and look to the future. Cheating will shortchange you. In order to stop cheating, you may need to start working harder, but you will reap the rewards of studying for the rest of your life.

Something to think about:

"Truth will last forever. But lies last only a moment" (Proverbs 12:19); "Good people hate what is false. But wicked people do shameful and disgraceful things" (Proverbs 13:5).

MY PERSONAL THOUGHTS AND ACTION STEPS:

_____

_____

_____

_____

_____

_____

_____

_____

_____

_____

_____

_____

_____

_____

_____

_____

_____

9

IT KILLS ME TO MAKE A COMMITMENT

My friend Tim is a senior in high school. He is a new Christian who desires a lifestyle of godliness. Until recently, Tim thought that his dad earned his living from a successful investment firm. Then Tim found out that his dad is a drug dealer.

Tim discovered the drugs while his parents were out of town, so he confronted them over the phone. The phone call was a terrible experience for Tim. His mother did all the talking because his father was too embarrassed. She tried to make Tim feel guilty by saying that his accusations would destroy the family. She tried to blame Tim for his father's actions, saying the only reason his dad sold drugs was to provide clothes, a car, and money for Tim's activities. She ended her tirade by assaulting him verbally for being "naive and impressionable" and for "blowing things out of proportion."

With tears in his eyes, Tim told his parents that he didn't want illegal money, nor would he live in a house that was an outlet for drugs. His parents angrily told him never to return home. They said they were going to move without telling him where they were going.

Tim found out that his dad is a drug dealer.

Tim loves his parents, but he doesn't love what they're doing. He's making a commitment not to get involved in their lifestyle. He wants to honor his parents, but he cannot honor their actions. As you can imagine, the conflict is tearing him apart. He has been cut off from his family, which is his lifeline of support. Some have told him, "Who cares what they're doing; they're still your family." But for Tim, going back home would be a total compromise of his belief system.

Tim's maturity amazes me! While his mom is sacrificing her family for the rewards of wealth and lifestyle, this 17-year-old is standing firm in his commitment to be a man of God. God will bless his commitment and Tim will be a better person as a result of his commitment.

Tim's story illustrates how making a commitment to follow Christ is not always an experience filled with laughter and good times. It's all too easy for us to compromise what we believe so we can blend in with the crowd. Making a commitment is much tougher. My hope, as well as Tim's, is that when the tough times hit, you will be even tougher and make a commitment to do what is honorable.

Something to think about:

"In this world you will have trouble. But be brave! I [Jesus] have defeated the world!" (John 16:33).

MY
PERSONAL
THOUGHTS
AND
ACTION
STEPS:

10

CONFRONTING CONFLICT

Two girls in my youth group who were best friends last year won't even talk to each other this year. They were very close until things started going wrong in their relationship. They didn't understand that all quality relationships go through problems. I tried to explain to them that the strength of a relationship is revealed in how we deal with these problems.

All relationships experience tension. But many times the tension grows into conflict and trauma because we don't know how—nor do we take the time—to deal with tension when it raises its ugly head. Instead, we overreact and make irrational decisions and statements which we later regret. Most of us would rather eat liver than deal with tension. We keep our feelings buried inside without letting anyone know what we are experiencing. This style of managing conflict doesn't reduce tension, nor does it produce positive development in our relationships.

Conflict arises for various reasons: jealousy, gossip, self-centeredness, possessiveness, personality clashes, and even simple misunderstandings. No matter what the reasons are, a conflict must be dealt with in a

Most of us would rather eat liver than deal with tension.

manner aimed at saving the relationship. When we don't take the time to resolve relationship conflicts, we usually suffer painful consequences. We end up carrying our bad feelings while the person we are in conflict with often doesn't even know our feelings. Unresolved conflict has a way of internally affecting us and keeping us from doing what God wants us to do.

No one is free from conflict, not even the great men in the Bible. Conflict began in the Garden of Eden (Genesis 3) and has permeated human relationships ever since: Cain and Abel (Genesis 4); the people in Noah's day (Genesis 6); the Tower of Babel (Genesis 11); Paul and Barnabas (Acts 15). Even Jesus, the Prince of Peace, was involved in conflicts. Jesus started conflicts (Matthew 21:12-15), He helped resolve conflicts (John 8:3-11), and He avoided conflicts (Luke 4:28-30). Yet in spite of conflicts, He continued to have a world-changing ministry.

All conflicts have a beginning. This is where you first experience tension. You feel hurt, betrayed, or misunderstood. You try to figure out why you feel the way

Ask yourself, "Is this my fault?"

you do. You ask yourself, "Is this my fault? Do I have the right to be feeling this way? What did I do to deserve this?" This is the best time to resolve your conflict by asking these questions of the other person. If you don't solve the problem immediately, you begin to think of ways to put down the other person or get even. This is when anger begins to build up toward a great explosion.

The method of controlling conflict is confrontation—spending time with the other person to talk about the conflict. Confrontation should take place in a sensitive manner, allowing both of you to express and explain your feelings. If there is already too much ammunition stored up, there's a good chance that a "battle" will erupt, and defensiveness and separation will join in the war. But when it's done correctly, confrontation will eventually cause the other person either to blow off the existing relationship or agree to deal with the conflict and make adjustments.

Both parties need to make adjustments during the confrontation and agree on changes and expectations. It's usually more beneficial for both of you to change a little so that conflict resolution is a team effort. Realize that you will probably still have some tender feelings about the conflict, especially if you were hurt. Your feelings are important, but make sure that the other person knows that you forgive him or her.

Conflict is painful! But confrontation is vital or the pain will just get worse. It's a difficult path, but it's the right path to take if you want to experience the joy that God has made available through quality relationships.

Something to think about:

"When you are angry, do not sin. And do not go on being angry all day. Do not give the devil a way to defeat you" (Ephesians 4:26-27).

> **MY PERSONAL THOUGHTS AND ACTION STEPS:**
>
> _____
> _____
> _____
> _____
> _____
> _____
>
> _____
>
> _____
> _____
> _____
> _____
> _____
> _____
> _____
> _____
> _____
> _____
> _____

11

TOO COOL TO LAUGH AT YOURSELF

Alan made the water polo team in his sophomore year in high school. Though he was excited to be on the team, he didn't get much playing time. After only two games he quit. Then Alan joined the cross-country team, but he quit within a month because he wasn't allowed to run varsity.

One day at church I was playing pick-up basketball with some guys. Tom was there, but he refused to join us. He said he was too tired, but the real reason he wouldn't play was because he didn't want to be embarrassed for not being very good. I've noticed since then that Tom won't try anything in which he doesn't excel.

I am concerned about people like Alan and Tom. They limit their participation only to the events and activities where they do well. Their goal is not participating, but impressing people and gaining a positive reputation. My concern is that these people limit themselves and miss out on many great adventures in life.

Adopt a "go for it" attitude when it comes to trying something new.

I stink at golf, but I enjoy playing because I get to spend time with my dad, who loves to play. People laugh at my singing voice, but I love to sing the "oldies but goodies" from the radio. I'm a slow runner, but I still run because I enjoy exercising and being outdoors to see the sunset, check out the birds, and watch little kids playing at the park.

I've tried to adopt a "go for it" attitude when it comes to trying something new. Who cares what people think when they see me fall off the unicycle I'm learning to ride? So what if someone sees the fear on my face when I jump off the cliff into the lake? If some things weren't scary, they wouldn't be as much fun. Does it make any difference if I get in shape for the triathalon and enjoy running it, but don't win? Not a bit. My goal isn't to prove that I'm cool because I'm willing to try new things. I've learned that if I allow what other people think to keep me from trying new adventures and activities, I'm going to live a pretty boring life on this exciting playground called earth.

If you can learn to laugh at yourself and not take your reputation too seriously, you'll be more willing to attempt new experiences. By always trying to impress others you miss out on some great chances for fun. Allow yourself to look stupid every once in awhile. Maybe you should play a nerd in a skit and have a blast wearing stupid clothes. If somebody thinks you're weird, so what? Build a tree swing and enjoy being a kid again. If somebody thinks you're juvenile, who cares? Try asking the question you've been afraid to ask because you thought you'd look stupid for not knowing the answer. What's the big deal? What's going to happen to you if you do these things? Will someone laugh? Will you lose your position on the reputation ladder? No problem. Loosen up

> *God looks at you differently than people do.*

a little, take a good look in the mirror, and laugh at yourself.

One of the most rewarding discoveries you can make is understanding that God looks at you differently than people do. God looks at your heart. If you feel the need to impress someone, why not impress God with your heart by loving others and being yourself? If you're always trying to develop a reputation that isn't even based on who you really are, by the time you get it you'll probably be too old to enjoy it. Work on being yourself and you'll find new rewards in life.

the heck
with my
reputation...

Something to think about:

"God does not see the same way people see. People look at the outside of a person, but the Lord looks at the heart" (1 Samuel 16:7).

MY PERSONAL THOUGHTS AND ACTION STEPS:	

12

COURAGE: SAYING NO WHEN OTHERS ARE SAYING YES

Though we don't consciously think about it, we use courage every day—to ask someone out, to be ourselves, to seek a raise, to be different, to act nice to people outside our crowd, to invite others to church. These are acts that take courage. Courage might be defined as the ability to say no when your friends say yes (or say yes when they say no). Courage gives us the ability to stand up for what we believe is right, Christian, and godly.

Some people act courageous when they really aren't. Guys who are physically strong and look tough aren't necessarily courageous. Some of them are wimps—lacking personal values—hiding behind a strong body. Many guys at the gym are much stronger than I am physically (which isn't saying much), but they are weak inside because their belief system is easily persuaded by the crowd. Girls are no different. Often those who seem to be popular and have it all together are wimpy followers rather than courageous leaders.

Often those who seem to be popular are wimpy followers rather than courageous leaders.

The Bible is filled with stories of people like you and me who exercised courage to make a difference in their period of history. Remember David fighting Goliath?

Hosea had courage to trust God and love the prostitute he was to marry. Moses courageously and boldly confronted Pharaoh to release the captive Israelites. These men were heroes simply because they depended on God and acted with courage.

The reason there are so many wimps and followers in the world is because it's easier than taking a stand. Being courageous is tough! But courage is available for those of us who are willing to take a stand. Our world needs fewer wimps and followers, and more people who will be courageous for what they believe.

Something to think about:

"Be strong and brave. Don't be afraid or worried because of the king of Assyria or his large army. There is a greater power with us than with him. He only has men, but we have the Lord our God" (2 Chronicles 32:7-8).

MY PERSONAL THOUGHTS AND ACTION STEPS:	

13

OPENING YOUR BAGGAGE ON A DATE

There is a side to dating that can be a real blast. But there's another dimension to dating that borders on being stressful. John wonders why Tracy doesn't like him as much as he likes her. Jason wants to stop dating Carla, but he's afraid it will destroy her. Tammy and Rick like each other, but neither wants to let the other one know.

There appears to be a simple truth at the root of the dating problems I hear about: Everyone has different expectations for a date or dating relationship. Some kids date for fun while others date to find a serious relationship. One may want to make out while the other wants to dance. The problem is that neither communicates his or her desire for the date. So each enters the date with an unspoken agenda and goes home disappointed that the other person didn't read his or her mind and respond accordingly.

When you go on a date, you are taking along 15, 16, or 17 (or however old you are) years of personal baggage. This baggage includes your value system, your needs, your

Each enters the date with an unspoken agenda.

dreams, your emotional hurts, your family experiences (good and bad), your faith, your outlook on life, your physical standards, etc. Your date also brings along his or her baggage, which is obviously different from yours to some degree. Your date's values, dreams, and

51

standards may be radically different from yours, or they may contrast only slightly. But there will be a difference. Each person's expectations for the date reflect who he or she is and the contents of his or her baggage.

People often have bad dating experiences because one or both partners don't share their expectations. They just go along for the ride with only one person's ideas being the schedule for the evening. I suggest that you take the pressure off your dating situations by taking time to express your expectations. Go on fun dates which allow time for interaction. If you go to movies all the time, you're only interacting with the popcorn and the screen, not your date.

If your date isn't interested in hearing and respecting your ideas and desires (your baggage), he or she isn't worth your time. Consider yourself valuable, share your thoughts, ideas, and dreams, and your date will begin to treat you with value.

Something to think about:

"Do your best to live in peace with everyone" (Romans 12:18).

MY
PERSONAL
THOUGHTS
AND
ACTION
STEPS:

_____
_____
_____
_____
_____
_____
_____
_____
_____
_____
_____
_____
_____
_____
_____
_____
_____
_____
_____
_____
_____
_____

14

WAITING FOR DATING IS NORMAL

Brandi was infatuated with Bill. She hoped that she had finally found a guy to date, someone who was caring, thoughtful, and fun. Bill's response to Brandi seemed to indicate that he was interested too. For several weeks they attended youth group activities together. These weren't official dates, but Bill and Brandi always managed to spend time together during each event.

The night before Brandi went on vacation, Bill hinted about dating her when she returned. That's all she needed to hear. While on vacation she sent him letters, bought him souvenirs, and thought about how great they would be together. When she returned two weeks later, Brandi's bubble burst. Bill had gotten involved with another girl in the group. Brandi was devastated.

Four months later Brandi asked three different guys to a school dance. All had apparently legitimate excuses to turn her down. Now what? She was zero for four in the dating game. Her .000 batting average might cause you to

"I thought I was the only person in the world who hasn't been on a date."

think that Brandi needed reconstructive surgery. But Brandi is an attractive young woman with a great personality and a zeal for life. She'll be a great catch for someone—someday.

Brandi's disappointing experience with dating is normal. There are millions of people who either don't date or can't get one. A few years ago I was shocked to learn that half of the adult population of the United States didn't date until after graduating from high school. When I revealed this statistic to the students in my group, they were relieved. One student responded, "I thought I was the only person in the world who hasn't been on a date."

I have a beautiful, red-haired friend named Syd who didn't date until her late 20s. Eventually, she met and married Darrell, and now they have kids and a happy family...even though she never dated in high school! Your dating experiences (or lack of them) during high school are no indication of how the rest of your life will be. There are people who dated every weekend during high school and never found happiness. Three marriages later they are still looking for Mr. or Ms. Right.

I realize that it's tough not to be dating when your friends are. There's a great deal of pressure today to be involved in a relationship. We base a degree of our self-worth on our success at attracting someone of the opposite sex. My hope is that you will realize that, if you don't date, you're not alone. Actually, you're in good company; there are many others in your same situation. If you're not dating, you're normal. God is still God, He's still on His throne, and His timing is perfect.

Something to think about:

"So don't worry, because I am with you. Don't be afraid, because I am your God. I will make you strong and will help you. I will support you with my right hand that saves you" (Isaiah 41:10).

MY PERSONAL THOUGHTS AND ACTION STEPS:

_____

_____

_____

_____

_____

_____

_____

_____

_____

_____

_____

_____

_____

_____

_____

_____

15

DIVORCE IS A DRAG!

So your parents are divorced? Join the crowd. About half of your friends are going through the same kinds of emotions and struggles you are. It isn't easy to experience the pain, loss, guilt, and frustration that goes along with being separated from someone you love. It's tough when the two people you love the most decide that they can't live together anymore. You may be distressed by thinking that the divorce was partly your fault. Again, you're not alone. Most kids from divorced homes feel that the breakup was the result of something they did. No matter how you look at it, divorce is a drag and it's very easy to hate divorce.

You may be comforted to know that God also hates divorce. He hates divorce because He knows the devastating pain it brings. You may be wondering, "Then where is God? If He loves me so much, why do I hurt so bad?" God wants to comfort you during your time of pain, but He's not necessarily going to take all your pain away. That's not how He works. Anybody who tells you to just believe God and all your troubles will be over is a liar. Personal growth comes through struggling and asking tough questions when God doesn't seem to be very near. We must believe that He *is* near like He promised to be, and that He *is*

> *God hates divorce because He knows the devastating pain it brings.*

57

working for our good in the pain of a divorce situation, even when the pain is still very real.

Let me illustrate this truth by talking about ice cream. You can decide whether you like a new flavor of ice cream by looking at it, smelling it, tasting it, and then saying, "It's good!" But with God it's different. You can't see Him, smell Him, or taste Him to decide whether He's good or not. Rather, we believe on the basis of Scripture that He is good, and as we trust in His goodness during the painful times in life, we begin to see the evidences of His comfort and love.

There is no doubt that divorce is a drag. As you trust God for comfort, begin to ask questions and seek out those who can relate to you and encourage you. Your pain will not disappear, but you will be comforted to know that you aren't alone.

Lord
I know you're good,
but it still hurts

Something to think about:

"God has also given us a desire to know the future. God certainly does everything at just the right time. But we can never completely understand what he is doing" (Ecclesiastes 3:11).

MY PERSONAL THOUGHTS AND ACTION STEPS:

_____

_____

_____

_____

_____

_____

_____

_____

_____

_____

_____

_____

_____

_____

_____

_____

_____

_____

16

IF GOD WAS LIKE THE ELECTRIC COMPANY

Frequently we perceive our ministers as super-spiritual people. We think that their calls to God are local, while ours are long-distance. But I'm a minister and I know better. You'd be surprised how many ministers miss their quiet times with God because they get too busy doing God's work. They lose sight of priorities and lack discipline with their time just like every other Christian. They ride that same spiritual roller coaster you do. They have just been on it longer and don't dip as often.

Staying disciplined with daily activities like Bible reading and prayer reminds me of paying bills. Last night I sat at my desk and paid bills. If I didn't pay the bills, my family would be in trouble. The electric company would shut off our lights, the bank would take away our car, and the water company would cut off our water. These consequences motivate me to pay my bills on time.

Sometimes I wish God would shut off His love to me when I

God doesn't threaten to shut off His love if we don't "pay our bills."

don't spend time with Him, or take away my eternal life when I don't pray. At least He could remind me with an audible voice when I blow it. That would motivate me. But He doesn't deal with us that way. He doesn't charge us for His love and threaten to shut it off if we don't "pay our bills" through our daily disciplines. God gives us His love, and our response of devotion to Him is strictly voluntary, based on our love for Him. He encourages our response and waits with open arms for whatever daily "payments" we lovingly send to Him.

Look at your own life. Do you appreciate the love and power which flows continually from God into your life? What kinds of loving payments are you making to God in return? Just like ministers, sometimes you will be disciplined and sometimes you will be apathetic. That's why Christianity is a process and not an overnight success. Whether you are ordained or not, your road to Christian maturity is being a disciplined follower of Him. Our God is always ready to receive your payments.

Something to think about:

"Examine and see how good the Lord is. Happy is the person who trusts the Lord" (Psalm 34:8).

MY PERSONAL THOUGHTS AND ACTION STEPS:

_____

_____

_____

_____

_____

_____

_____

_____

_____

_____

_____

_____

_____

_____

_____

_____

_____

_____

_____

17

I HAVE NO CONCERN FOR EMPATHY

I t seems like every year a fatal accident prematurely ends the life of a student at one of our nearby schools. People are shocked, hurt, and confused. The pain of such a loss most directly affects the immediate family, but it quickly ripples out to affect friends and acquaintances. Our youth group meetings which follow these tragedies are filled with conversation and questions: "What should we do? What should the church do? What should I do?" It's hard to know what to do.

There's no one answer that is going to be right for every situation, but communicating empathy is a great place to start. Empathy is possessing and showing genuine interest and concern in what is happening. It's a beautiful quality, one that is difficult to fake because empathy can often be seen in the eyes.

Some Christians think the best thing to do during a tragedy is to quote Scripture to those who are hurting, or tell them not to lose faith because everything is going to be okay. I'm not sure this really comforts those who hurt. I get angry when I read the Book of Job in the Old Testament and see how his friends treated him during his trials. While Job is emotionally destroyed over the loss of his family, his friends tell him he's not close enough to God,

Empathy usually communicates better than anything.

and that he better get back on the spiritual track or God will continue to punish him. I'm thankful that my theology—and my friends—aren't like that.

Nonverbal empathy usually communicates better than anything we can say. Maybe you just need to sit and hold her hand, or give him a hug and allow him to cry on your shoulder. If you feel the need to say something, you might say, "I'm not sure what to say right now, but I want you to know that I'm sorry, that I love you, and that I'm here if you need anything."

People around you are experiencing tragedies on a daily basis. Though some tragedies may appear trivial (like acne breaking out the day of a date), your empathy in all situations will communicate concern. It will also reveal God's love through you. Where there is empathy, there is support; where there is support, there is encouragement; and where there is encouragement, there is love. It's within the security of love that people will feel comforted, not because of what you say, but because of who you are—a messenger of God's powerful and accepting love.

Something to think about:

"The Lord God has put his Spirit in me. This is because he has appointed me to tell the good news to the poor. He has sent me to comfort those whose hearts are broken. He has sent me to tell the captives they are free. He has sent me to tell the prisoners that they are released. He has sent me to announce the time when the Lord will show his kindness and the time when our God will punish evil people. He has sent me to comfort all those who are sad" (Isaiah 61:1-2).

MY PERSONAL THOUGHTS AND ACTION STEPS:

_____
_____
_____
_____
_____

_____
_____
_____
_____
_____
_____
_____
_____
_____

18

POWER: LIVING IN THE FAST LANE

If the speed laws on our highways permitted it, I would drive a lot faster than I do. When I drive on level, empty roads, I fantasize about being a race car driver, and I crave the thrill of driving at high speeds. I know there are lots of people like me who love the feel of power they get behind the wheel when driving the fast lane. But it seems like there are even more of us who like to *live* at high speeds—in the fast lane of life. We are a generation of people who always have something going on.

Living in the fast lane produces certain kinds of stress that we might not experience if we didn't have so much going on. As a teenager, racing in the fast lane to stay ahead of home responsibilities, social life, relationships, sports, clubs, academics, and concerns for the future can really stress you out. Everyone reacts differently to stress, but when you're overwhelmed with stress, it's difficult to be the person God intended you to be. Stress keeps us worrying about how we are going to survive the

> *We are a generation of people who always have something going on.*

next pile of work, due date, report, or person in our life.

Those of us who are constantly living in the fast lane seem to be racing through life searching for something—and I think that something is acceptance. It amazes me that the busiest people I know (myself included) keep driving hard in life to prove themselves and get approval from others, whether they achieve it or not.

"So what?" you shrug. "I like being busy. I feel bored when I'm not busy, almost like I'm lazy, and I don't ever want to be known as a lazy person." When you travel in the fast lane, you don't take time to appreciate what's around you, because you are always looking ahead to make sure you don't run into something or run over someone. Many of us would do better to slow down, change lanes, and enjoy the view.

Something to think about:

"I have good plans for you. I don't plan to hurt you. I plan to give you hope and a good future. Then you will call my name. You will come to me and pray to me. And I will listen to you" (Jeremiah 29:11-12).

MY PERSONAL THOUGHTS AND ACTION STEPS:

19

I'M CONFIDENT THAT I'M FEARFUL

Lately, I've been doing a lot of traveling in airplanes. I feel comfortable in planes and rarely think of air tragedies. But one recent Monday morning was different. I was in Mexico City waiting to board my flight, which was an hour and a half behind schedule due to mechanical problems. I tried to determine the problem by watching the mechanics work on the plane. The gate agent would only say that the plane was experiencing "minor difficulties."

When we finally got into the air, the pilot announced that the plane was leaking fuel and that we were going to have to land early. As I tried to take my mind off the fuel problem, we flew into some turbulence that shook the plane badly. I tried to convince myself that I wasn't nervous by reading the newspaper. But suddenly my eyes focused on a headline that read: "Plane Crash Kills 78 People." That did it. I became very nervous and feared for my life. But, of course, everything ended well and I lived to write about it.

Fearing for our lives isn't a typical daily concern. We have other types of fear which seem to attack us on a daily basis. Barbara fears what other people will think and say about her. Tim is scared about the first day of school. Greg is nervous about his public speaking presentation. Katy is

> *God has the power to minimize our fears.*

fearful of what her friends will think of her new style of clothes. Diane is paranoid about being ridiculed for her new perm. Carl is uneasy about being seen with his mom at the football game. It's these types of fears that continually enter our lives.

It seems as though Peter, one of the heroes of the Bible, experienced both the fear of dying and the fear of rejection. He feared for his life when walking to Jesus on the water. And he was also fearful when others associated him with Jesus during His trial. He feared rejection so much that he denied knowing Jesus at least three times.

None of us are alone when it comes to being afraid. That's why the Bible has given us direction in this area. Jesus repeatedly encourages us not to be afraid by promising that He will always be with us and never leave us. Paul spoke to our fears by reminding us that we can do all things through the strength of Christ. The Christians I see who aren't very fearful over little things display a special quality in their lives. It's a mark of Christian maturity which displays confidence in the power and presence of God in their lives. These people know the biblical promises, understand them, and are sure that the God who reigns in their lives has the power to minimize their fears.

Remember, as a little kid, you would taunt, "My father is stronger than your father, so ha-ha"? You felt confident that you could conquer the world with your dad on your side. Well, it's even more true with your Heavenly Father. There's no one more powerful. When we really sense God's power and presence, we maximize our confidence and minimize our fears.

Something to think about:

"The Lord himself will go before you. He will be with you. He will not leave you or forget you. Don't be afraid. Don't worry" (Deuteronomy 31:8).

> **MY PERSONAL THOUGHTS AND ACTION STEPS:**
>
> _____
>
> _____
>
> _____
>
> _____
>
> _____
>
> _____
>
> _____
>
> _____
>
> _____
>
> _____
>
> _____
>
> _____
>
> _____
>
> _____
>
> _____
>
> _____

20

FLOSSING AWAY SELF-HATRED

Recently, I went to the dentist to get my teeth cleaned. I hated it! It had been years since I went last, and I paid a sore price. Not only did I bleed and salivate all over the dentist's fingers, but I was in pain from all the pressure she put on my gums. But the pain in my mouth was mild compared to the painful scolding I received for not flossing. The dentist told me that food gets trapped between my teeth, and it cannot be reached by a toothbrush. This food turns into bacteria which releases a destructive acid. She warned that if I don't remove the bacteria-producing particles by flossing regularly, my gums will rot and stop supplying nourishment to my teeth, which will eventually fall out.

On my way home from the dentist's office, I did two things. First, I bought some dental floss; I was converted! Second, I began to think about the implications of flossing in other areas of our lives. Different influences enter our lives on a daily basis. Many of these are negative. We are told that we aren't good enough, thin enough, pretty enough, smart enough, nice enough, or talented enough. Since these comments aren't true, we swallow them with disregard. But it seems like every day at least one negative

It seems like every day at least one negative comment "sticks between our teeth."

comment "sticks between our teeth." These negative remarks turn into bacteria which eventually release the acid of self-hatred. This acid rots our view of life and the way we look at ourselves. It becomes a disease that infests our vision, causing us to see little good in ourselves.

The dentist tells us to clean our teeth through routine brushing. In life, our routine brushing consists of the positive comments we receive each day. We may be told that our hair looks nice, our clothes are stylish, or our jokes are funny. This routine praise is nice, but it's like normal brushing which doesn't destroy all the bacteria. We need to floss.

I see flossing as the daily realization that we were created by God. We were formed in His own image. God knew what we were going to look like before we were born. What an awesome thought! God cares about us this much! My hope is that you realize the power behind God's love and acceptance. Recognizing and appreciating this truth on a daily basis is the only thing that will destroy the acid of self-hatred.

Something to think about:

"You made my whole being. You formed me in my mother's body. I praise you because you made me in an amazing and wonderful way. What you have done is wonderful. I know this very well. You saw my bones being formed as I took shape in my mother's body. When I was put together there, you saw my body as it was formed. All the days planned for me were written in your book before I was one day old" (Psalm 139:13-16).

MY
PERSONAL
THOUGHTS
AND
ACTION
STEPS:

_____

_____

_____

_____

_____

_____

_____

_____

_____

_____

_____

_____

_____

_____

THE F.O.G. CAN MAKE IT CLEAR

It seems like every ordinary day bombards us with hundreds of decisions which need to be made. These decisions begin the moment we wake up: "Should I throw my alarm against the wall? What should I wear? What should I eat? How am I going to get to school? Should I throw my sandwich at the freshman riding his bike? Should I go to my locker before first period?" Though these are minor decisions, our ability to deal with them on a daily basis affects our ability to deal with larger decisions throughout our lives. For example, how do you make decisions when it comes to your family, your friends, or your sexual standards? Do you think about them? Just make them? Pray about them? Draw straws for options? Consult stuffed animals? How do you make your decisions, large or small?

> **Feelings.**
> **Others.**
> **God.**

I was driving back from the river one day with my car filled with high school students. It was very foggy out, and I was driving slowly and cautiously. The fog was so bad in spots I couldn't even see the center divider, so I had to open the door to make sure where it was. Finally, we decided to stop at a dumpy-looking diner until the fog cleared. For the next two hours we talked about the pain of making decisions. Ironically, we came up with a formula for decision-making using the letters F.O.G. Obviously, the F.O.G. formula may not work for all your situations, but it's easy to remember and worth trying.

Feelings: We have an emotional side to us that reacts when we are faced with decisions. How do you feel when you think about the consequences of your decision? What is your gut-level feeling? If you had to make the decision right now based on your feelings, what would it be? Mandy wanted to talk about how her boyfriend was pressuring her toward sexual activity. When I asked her how she felt about being pressured, she responded, "When I *think* about it, I really want to go out with him and 'do it.' But I just don't *feel* right about it." The more we explored her feelings, the better she felt about deciding not to get involved sexually.

Others: When you need to make a decision, surround yourself with wise people. Others can look at the question more objectively, and they don't have as much emotional energy invested in the decision as you do. The Bible says that in the counsel of many

> *When driving in the fog, slow down and drive defensively.*

people there is wisdom. Ask opinions and weigh the advice given. But be careful whom you ask. You may ask someone who wants your girlfriend if you should jump off a bridge, and he's likely to make you think it's a good idea. Find people you trust.

God: Obviously, God shouldn't be the last one consulted. But if He was first in this acronym it would spell G.O.F., which doesn't make sense. God desires to be invited into your decision-making. He wants to be an active part of your life's game plan, and He will guide you through your decisions if you're willing to listen to Him.

When driving in the fog it's usually best to slow down and drive defensively. The same is true when the fog of life rolls in and you're confused or blinded about the implications of your decisions. It's time to slow down and pull over. Examine how you really feel, seek the counsel and wisdom of others, and share your thoughts with your caring Father who wants the very best for you. Drive safely.

Something to think about:

"Trust the Lord with all your heart. Don't depend on your own understanding. Remember the Lord in everything you do. And he will give you success" (Proverbs 3:5-6).

MY PERSONAL THOUGHTS AND ACTION STEPS:

_____

_____

_____

_____

_____

_____

_____

_____

_____

_____

22

LIVING AHEAD OF YOURSELF

A few weeks ago Cathy and I had dinner with three eighth-grade girls. I was surprised that the main topic of our conversation was college. They were concerned about getting accepted, what their SAT scores would be, and if their parents would be able to pay for school. They were talking about how great it will be to live on their own, to go to school when they want, to not have a curfew, and to be completely independent.

I couldn't believe it! I realize that college is important, but I felt like saying, "How about reaching puberty before reaching for college applications? You girls are still two years away from getting your driver's licenses." I wanted to remind them of the joys associated with the present.

We continually look to the future for our happiness. When

We continually look to the future for our happiness.

we play this game of living in the future, we forget about the gift of today. The problem is that we can only anticipate what the future will be like. We forget that every day we live is a miracle in itself. God has given us everything we need to be happy. Sure, it's great to dream and plan, but when we allow the future to keep us from dealing with the gift of today, we are living ahead of ourselves.

Something to think about:

"So I tell you, don't worry about the food you need to live. And don't worry about the clothes you need for your body. Life is more important than food. And the body is more important than clothes.... You cannot add any time to your life by worrying about it" (Matthew 6:25,27).

MY
PERSONAL
THOUGHTS
AND
ACTION
STEPS:

_____

_____

_____

_____

_____

_____

_____

_____

_____

_____

_____

_____

_____

_____

_____

_____

23

FATHER'S DAY EVERY DAY

For Eileen, Father's Day is a painful holiday. Her father left her when she was two years old. Since then she's had three stepfathers. The first two had sex with her before she was 12 years old. Her present stepfather seems like a great guy, but she can't bring herself to trust him or show any affection to him. As a 16-year-old, Eileen lives in fear that he will be no different from the others.

Maybe you can relate to Eileen's pain. There are millions of people who have had negative experiences with their fathers. The pain is unbelievable. It's also painful for you to go to church and hear God referred to as Father. You have a difficult time understanding how God the Father can love you, because the memories of your father are so painful. Having a negative relationship with your earthly father has affected your ability to surrender to Father God.

It would be silly of me to think that I can solve your pain in a short devotional. But I can share an idea about how you

Find help in dealing with the pain of your earthly father as you grow in your relationship with God the Father.

can understand God the Father better. It is beyond us to comprehend a Father who is so loving, caring, and unique as our God. My hope is that you will find help in dealing with the pain of your earthly father as you grow in your relationship with God the Father, who will never leave you nor forsake you.

God the Father is your Creator. You may be the biological son or daughter of your earthly parents, but God is the Creator of all of life. God spoke into existence this incredible playground we call earth. He created us to know Him and fellowship with Him. His anticipation for His children to know Him is inconceivable. I know the feelings of an expectant father who can't wait to see his child, and who longs for the day when the child will say, "I love you." The Bible tells us that God saw you and loved you while you were still in your mother's womb. Now that's love only a Creator can have!

God the Father is your Comforter. God is the God of concern. He hurts when you hurt. When Jesus ascended into heaven, God gave us His Holy Spirit as a Comforter. His forgiveness is the fruit of His comforting nature. He

> *God the Father wants to know you, love you, and grow you.*

wants to forgive us so we can live free of bondage. All through the New Testament we see illustrations of God's personality through the actions of Jesus, the God-man. His acts were acts of compassion performed to bring comfort to those who hurt. God is concerned about you and your pain.

God the Father is a challenger. God challenges us to grow and to be mature. He wants us to do something with the knowledge we have. Three times He asked His disciple Peter, "Do you love me?" All three times Peter responded by saying, "Yes." Jesus then told him to feed and care for His sheep. Jesus was calling Peter to action, something He continually does with those He loves. When He washed the disciples' feet at the dinner table, He told them to serve others in the same way. God the Father loves us enough to challenge us to make our lives count by helping others.

God the Father wants to know you, love you, and grow you. If you can't allow that to happen because of your painful relationship with your earthly father, please talk with someone who can help you. You're not alone. God the Father understands. He created you, and now He wants to help you.

Something to think about:

"Praise be to the God and Father of our Lord Jesus Christ. God is the Father who is full of mercy. And he is the God of all comfort. He comforts us every time we have trouble, so that we can comfort others when they have trouble. We can comfort them with the same comfort that God gives us" (2 Corinthians 1:3-4).

MY PERSONAL THOUGHTS AND ACTION STEPS:

_____

_____

_____

_____

_____

_____

_____

_____

_____

_____

_____

_____

_____

_____

24

TRAINING YOUR PARENTS BY TRADING GREED FOR GRACE

I have yet to meet a family where the members have perfect relationships with each other. All families have some form of parent/child problems. And many homes have become war zones because of family disagreements and the way the parents and teenagers people treat each other.

Linda was having trouble with her family, so they asked me to "fix" her. At our first meeting, I asked Linda what she wanted to change about herself to help the situation. She told me she didn't want to change anything. "My parents are the ones who need to do all the changing," she announced. Her thinking was not only immature, it was stupid. Most people know that for any type of relational healing to take place there needs to be cooperation on both sides. I kept pressing Linda about her plans to change. She continued to refuse, so I walked her out the door and told her I couldn't do a thing if she wasn't willing to change at all. One of the first steps toward healing a bad relationship with parents is to be willing to change yourself.

> *There needs to be cooperation on both sides.*

A second step is to understand what parents are going through. Your parents don't have it easy. They don't have college degrees in parenting. They're not professional parents. They have lots of responsibilities in caring for you along with their careers and personal life. In addition to their responsibilities, they have strong personal emotions to deal with: feelings of failure in their disciplines, feelings associated with getting older, feelings of inadequacy in their own relationships. On top of all this, they're parents of adolescents—and that scares them to death. They know about the horror stories of substance abuse (more than 10,000 deaths each year; over two million teenage alcoholics), sexual activity (in the 1960s, ten percent of adolescents were sexually active; today it's over 60 percent), abortions, suicides, violence, crime, eating disorders, self-hatred, runaways, and school dropouts. Can you imagine living with this much pressure? I've had parents tell me that they feel successful if they do a good job of parenting only 25 to 50 percent of the time.

What your parents need from you is a little grace. By grace, I mean allowing them the freedom to fail without verbally abusing them. Cut them a little slack. Your

Cut your parents a little slack.

loving behavior will blow them away, since they are conditioned for greed—always hearing you ask for the things you want. Try giving your parents some options so all their decisions aren't reactions against your ultimatums. Don't be so emotionally reactionary (like running to your room yelling "I hate you") when your parents upset you.

Responsible behavior is more likely to get you the freedom you want. Acting mature with your parents is the best way to show them grace and gain their respect. Allow your parents to know you love them and are concerned about them.

Something to think about:

"Why do you notice the little piece of dust that is in your brother's eye, but you don't notice the big piece of wood that is in your own eye? Why do you say to your brother, 'Let me take that little piece of dust out of your eye'? Look at yourself first! You still have that big piece of wood in your own eye. You are a hypocrite! First, take the wood out of your own eye. Then you will see clearly enough to take the dust out of your brother's eye" (Matthew 7:3-5).

MY PERSONAL THOUGHTS AND ACTION STEPS:
_____
_____
_____
_____
_____
_____
_____
_____
_____
_____
_____
_____

25

NO, THANKS, I'D RATHER BE UNGRATEFUL

An important component of personal joy and peace is found in our ability to be thankful. Unfortunately, we live in a world where few people express thankfulness. We play the "when-then" game: *"When* I get my driver's license, *then* I'll be happy"; *"When* I find a boyfriend, *then* I'll be thankful"; *"When* I am accepted into college, *then* I'll be grateful for my present education." By comparing ourselves to others and wishing we had more than we do, we overlook the things we have which require our gratitude.

Thankfulness is an attitude of gratitude for what we have been given. It comes when we realize how fortunate we are to be alive and able to participate in the luxuries of this world. If you have a hard time being thankful, I encourage you to

> *Look beyond your back-yard and see how others in this world live.*

look beyond your backyard and see how others in this world live. Then begin listing all the reasons you have to be thankful.

Recently, 20 of our students returned from a trip to Haiti, the poorest country in the western hemisphere. The first thing they described to me as they stepped off the plane was their new awareness of how much they have been given. And whenever our youth group drives into Mexico and sees five-member families living in cardboard shacks, we quickly realize how much we take for granted. We have so much to be thankful for!

Once we realize what we have, we can express gratitude to God through seeking His will for our lives, hard work, patience, laughter, creativity, persistence, loving, and caring for others. We can thank God by sharing our faith, and by not taking Him, other people, or our possessions— no matter how limited they may be—for granted.

The following lines describe a man who learned to be thankful:

The Unknown Confederate Soldier

I asked God for strength that I might achieve; I was made weak that I might learn humbly to obey.

I asked God for health that I might do great things; I was given infirmity that I might do better things.

I asked for riches that I might be happy; I was given poverty that I might be wise.

I asked for power that I might have the praise of men; I was given weakness that I might feel the need of God.

I asked for all things that I might enjoy life; I was given life that I might enjoy all things.

Almost despite myself my unspoken prayers were answered.

I am among all men most richly blessed.

Something to think about:

"Give thanks whatever happens. That is what God wants for you in Christ Jesus" (1 Thessalonians 5:18).

MY PERSONAL THOUGHTS AND ACTION STEPS:

_____

_____

_____

_____

_____

_____

_____

_____

_____

_____

_____

_____

_____

_____

_____

_____

_____

_____

_____

_____

26

STRESSING OUT OR GROWING UP

I don't know much about weightlifting, but I understand the basic physiology of muscle growth. Growth happens as a muscle encounters stress when performing a specific exercise with a heavy weight. Through exercise, the stress of the weight causes the muscle cells to tear or break down. When the damaged cells are given time to rest, they repair themselves and grow larger, which increases the size of the muscle.

Doesn't it seem strange that stress causes growth? Do you think the same principle can apply to us as persons? Can the stress in our lives actually produce growth? I realize that many adults don't think your stress as a teenager compares to theirs. Some think that what you call stress isn't real stress at all. But the stress you face at your age is intense. It occurs as you try to achieve and prove yourself in school, work to fit in with friends, improve your physical appearance, figure out how to live with your family, deal with too much freedom or not enough freedom, and plan for your future. Stress is real, and

> *Stress can either bury you or boost you.*

it's frustrating, tiring, and downright painful.
Your stress can either bury you or boost you into a new level of growth, understanding, and maturity. Your life is similar to that of a muscle. Stress won't produce growth if you don't take time to catch your breath, rest, and try

to learn from what you have been through. If we continually overload our lives, taking on more and more activity in hopes that we will become better, more popular, or smarter, the result will be fatigue, frustration, and anger. I've seen dozens of young people who are exhausted, ready to break and throw in the towel on life. They've allowed stress to overwhelm them and life becomes too much to bear.

If you feel like you're about to be buried under a pile of stress, try slowing down. Drop some of your extracurricular activities. Learn to say no, stop trying to prove yourself, and ask for help. Talk with someone who is older and wiser about your activities, rethink your time and priorities, read Scripture, and ask God for insight into a new direction. Ask yourself, "What is the worst thing that could happen if I stopped stressing out over this?" If you discover that the world isn't going to stop turning, and that you'll still be alive tomorrow, maybe it's time to take the pressure off yourself.

Everyone has stress and goes through tough times. But you can use stress as an exercise device to become a stronger person. When it's about to bury you, step aside, evaluate it, and learn from what you've been through.

Something to think about:

"Come to me, all of you who are tired and have heavy loads. I will give you rest. Accept my work and learn from me. I am gentle and humble in spirit. And you will find rest for your souls" (Matthew 11:28-29).

MY PERSONAL THOUGHTS AND ACTION STEPS:

27

SEEING THE BIG PICTURE: GROWING UP AND MOVING ON

I love graduation parties—people, fun, food, and laughter. I also get a kick from listening to the idealism of the graduates. Each graduating class believes it is going to be a major force in the world, and that the world will revolve around the gifts of its members. I love to hear their plans and dreams, and I pray that every new graduate is able to do what he wants to do. But the problem I see with many graduates is that they are looking for the next party instead of the next opportunity. They move from party to party looking for happiness, acceptance, and truth. It may take some time, but each of them eventually realizes that he or she will have to grow up.

Tyler is excited about getting out of high school and moving on with life. But I'm concerned about Tyler because I know he's not adequately prepared for the real world. Contrary to what Tyler (or any other idealistic graduate) thinks, the world doesn't revolve around him, nor is it slowing down to wait for him to graduate. It bothers me that he can't see "the big picture."

They are looking for the next party instead of the next opportunity.

The big picture for Tyler is this: As a Christian, he

needs to see his life in terms of how God fits into every activity and relationship, not how much fun he can have. Being a Christian should affect everything he does, both in high school and in the great world beyond. Maturity is allowing Christ to make a difference in all areas of our lives. But Tyler and other Christian graduates are not ready to make a difference for Christ in the world if they are not making a difference for Him in their lives right now—school, sports, parents, friends, personal qualities, and dreams for the future.

Seeing the big picture is looking past high school and seeing where God fits into every area of your life to come. Ask yourself, "What do I want my faith to be like ten years from now?" Realize that the decisions you make about involving Christ in your life today will affect the rest of your life. Do what it takes right now to commit to that image. Surround yourself with the right crowd, people who will support you in your godly goals. Get serious about your faith now and allow Christ to have impact in the big picture of your life today.

Something to think about:

"God has made us what we are. In Christ Jesus, God made us new people so that we would do good works. God had planned in advance those good works for us. He had planned for us to live our lives doing them" (Ephesians 2:10).

MY PERSONAL THOUGHTS AND ACTION STEPS:	_____
	_____
	_____
	_____
	_____

_____

_____

_____

_____

_____

_____

_____

_____

_____

_____

_____

28

FOR GUYS ONLY: HOW LONG WILL GIRLS PLAY ALONG?

It's not unusual for guys to be consumed with girls. What *is* unusual is the way guys often treat girls. Though many guys tell me they're looking for a girl who is more than a puppet (someone who will do what they say), their actions don't match their words.

When a guy moves beyond the stage of thinking about girls only in physical terms, he looks for a girl who thinks for herself and who is willing to stand up for what she believes. This is an admirable quest, but I don't see these guys treating girls much differently from those who are interested only in a girl's body. When are guys going to start treating girls as respectable individuals instead of objects of their desires? A girl's desire for acceptance will often lead her to give in to a guy's physical desires, hoping her cooperation will gain her love and respect from him.

Laurie is a perfect example. She would do anything to get Bill's attention and affection—and she did. Two weeks after Bill got what he wanted, he broke up with her. Unfortunately, this kind of heartbreak happens all the time.

Treat girls as respectable individuals instead of objects of your desires.

Why is it that guys often have no idea how poorly they treat girls? Or do they have an idea, but don't care enough to stop misusing girls? It's frightening to think

96

that my baby daughter will grow up in a society of guys who will view her and treat her as an object instead of a person. My prayer is that this pattern will change before she becomes a teenager. Can you do anything to help?

Something to think about:

"Love each other like brothers and sisters. Give your brothers and sisters more honor than you want for yourselves" (Romans 12:10).

MY PERSONAL THOUGHTS AND ACTION STEPS:

_____

_____

_____

_____

_____

_____

_____

_____

_____

_____

_____

_____

_____

_____

_____

_____

29

HAVE YOU FOUND A H.A.T. THAT FITS YOU?

Recently, when speaking at a seminar in Seattle, I met a freckle-faced, red-haired student. He looked so "All-American" that he could have been from Richie Cunningham's family. He approached me with tears in his eyes after one session and struggled to say these words: "I liked what you had to say, but I'm frustrated because I'm not sure I know who I am. I seem to be a different person for each situation I'm in."

We can all relate to his statement. Even though God created each of us as one person, we seem to portray several identities and play several roles. We play the role of the child when we are with our parents, we play the student while at school, we are jocks when with our athletic team, etc. I'm sure you could list 15 different roles you play throughout the week, each tailored to fit the particular crowd you are "playing" to.

As I talked with my young friend in Seattle, we decided that we play different roles because we are searching for something as we move from crowd to crowd. Somehow we think our role-playing will help us find these things. We listed several items people are looking for, but the three biggies were:

> *"I seem to be a different person for each situation I'm in."*

Happiness: Isn't it true that we want to be happy? Being joyful, having few problems, smiling a lot, laughing, and enjoying good times is the reward we want out of life. We think our search would be successful if we could find continual happiness.

Acceptance: It would be a dream come true if we could act the way we want to act and really be ourselves, and still be accepted by everyone. Wouldn't that be great?

Truth: We have so many questions that we need and want answers to. If only we could find the truth about all we want to know, our search would be over.

As I thought about these three words I recognized that their first letters spell *hat*. That little acronym can be very helpful to you. Whenever you put on a different "hat" by changing roles, you are searching for your H.A.T.—some form of happiness, acceptance, and truth. But in reality, your role-changing search will continue unfulfilled forever until you discover that there is only one hat you can wear to truly find your H.A.T. It's the hat God gives you when you realize that your relationship with Him is the answer to your search. His H.A.T. is a little different: It's a crown which symbolizes our royalty in His eyes. Find your identity in Him, then hold onto your H.A.T. and wear it with pride.

Something to think about:

"Now, a crown is waiting for me. I will get that crown for being right with God. The Lord is the judge who judges rightly, and he will give me the crown on that Day. He will give that crown not only to me but to all those who have waited with love for him to come again" (2 Timothy 4:8); "Then when Christ, the Head Shepherd, comes, you will get a crown. This crown will be glorious, and it will never lose its beauty" (1 Peter 5:4).

MY PERSONAL THOUGHTS AND ACTION STEPS:

_____

_____

_____

_____

_____

_____

_____

_____

_____

_____

_____

_____

_____

30

THE SUCCESS OF TELLING OTHERS YOU FAILED

One Sunday morning, Willie stopped me as I was entering a staff meeting. "I really need to talk to you," he said. I told him I would talk to him after Sunday school, but I was called out on an emergency so we didn't get the chance then. That afternoon he came to my house, but he didn't want to talk because a bunch of guys were there playing basketball. Later that night Willie and I finally got together after the evening's program, and he looked relieved.

Willie talked slowly with his drooping chin touching his chest. "I want you to know that I really blew it a few weeks ago. Me and a few of my non-Christian buddies went drinking. I had nine beers and got smashed. The reason I did it was because I was disillusioned with my faith and I wanted to rebel just to be bad. Last week at camp I realized that getting drunk was just a way to hide from what I really need to deal with. I know getting drunk is no big deal with most high school students, but I felt like I needed to tell someone that cared about me so I could

> *I've been feeling paralyzed by the guilt.*

move on in my relationship with Christ. I've been feeling paralyzed by the guilt, but now I'm ready to move on. I feel a lot better just telling you. Thanks."

What Willie did took guts. He didn't need to tell me

he blew it. He had already confessed his mistake and been forgiven by God. Forgiveness is God's job, not mine, and God's forgiveness is a biblical promise. So why did Willie tell me about his problem? Because there's something about confessing our failures to someone in addition to God which helps in the healing of guilt. There is power in sharing faults with another human. It's the positive feeling of expressing fault and still being accepted. It's comforting when a confession of guilt isn't followed by a black eye. It's cleansing to express a failure and then have a Christian friend put his arm around you and say, "It's okay; failure is just a part of growing in Christ."

There's no doubt that God designed us to hear each other's confessions of failure and affirm each other's forgiveness and worth. Comfort is available to each of us through the body of Christ.

Something to think about:

"But if we confess our sins, he will forgive our sins. We can trust God. He does what is right. He will make us clean from all the wrongs we have done" (1 John 1:9); "Confess your sins to each other and pray for each other. Do this so that God can heal you. When a good man prays, great things happen" (James 5:16).

MY PERSONAL THOUGHTS AND ACTION STEPS:	

31

NO ONE WILL EVER KNOW

Gavin and I were in the supermarket recently shopping for the church barbecue. When we walked down the bulk food aisle, he reached into a candy bin, grabbed a piece of candy, unwrapped it, and popped it into his mouth. When I asked him what he was doing, he said, "It's no big deal. How's a huge store like this going to miss one little piece of candy?"

Rick was talking about his new job and describing how his friend at work, who writes the checks, doubles Rick's paycheck. Instead of getting paid for the 20 hours he works each week, Rick gets paid for 40 hours. When I confronted him on the issue, Rick said, "The company is funded by a research grant. If my boss doesn't spend all the money he receives, he won't be given more money for the next research project. I'm just helping him spend the money faster. I'm sure if he knew, he wouldn't care."

Isn't it amazing how easily we can justify our questionable actions? And it seems like the more dishonest we are, the more believable our reasoning seems to us. We live in a world where the lack of integrity is as common as a newspaper. The Christian community also struggles with this problem. It's not unusual to hear about Christians stealing,

Isn't it amazing how easily we can justify our questionable actions?

carrying on illicit affairs, and cheating on business deals.

Integrity is synonymous with terms such as honesty, trustworthiness, loyalty, and faithfulness. We are faced with daily decisions which require us to choose between right and wrong, telling the truth or lying, and keeping or exposing secrets. These decisions can be hard, especially since we are so easily influenced by our society's declining moral standards. Someone who possesses the character qualities related to integrity is to be admired.

One day I faced three decisions which forced me to draw from my growing well of integrity. In the morning I discovered that someone had paid me $15.00 more in a transaction than he owed me. For a few brief moments I thought about keeping the extra cash by rationalizing the mistake as his fault.

Later that morning I discovered that my car stereo had been stolen. My insurance agent told me simply to turn in a list of the items which had been stolen and the company would send me a check for that amount. I thought, "Hey, I could claim all kinds of things that weren't actually stolen.

We are so easily influenced by our society's declining moral standards.

And I could add a hundred dollars to the price of the stereo and they would never know." I tried to justify my dishonest thoughts by telling myself that I had been ripped off, so why not rip someone else off? It would have been easy to do.

That night Cathy and I went to the cinema complex to see an early movie. When it was over, we bumped into friends in the lobby who were just arriving to see another movie in the complex. They suggested that we slip into the auditorium with them, since no one was checking ticket stubs. This was another integrity decision, because we only paid to see one movie.

Take a minute to think about all the daily decisions you make dealing with truth. They aren't always easy decisions, and we don't always make the right choices. I know *I* don't! My day with those three decisions didn't go perfectly. I blew it on one of my decisions, and I felt guilty afterwards because I knew what I did was wrong even before I did it. And as it turned out, the second movie wasn't very good anyway.

It's difficult to always make the right decisions. But as Christians, we should pursue Christ's example. Jesus spoke clearly about integrity in Matthew 5:37: "Say only 'yes' if you mean 'yes,' and say only 'no' if you mean 'no.' " In other words, speak the truth so you can be trusted.

The struggle to maintain integrity is common. Here's one way you can succeed in the struggle. Invite someone to hold you accountable to your commitment to integrity. Find a friend to be your integrity beeper, and be an integrity beeper for him. Every time one of you "forgets" the truth, the other person makes a beeping sound to remind you of your new commitment. An integrity beeper may help you grow to be the honest man or woman that God intends you to be.

Something to think about:

"He who follows the true way comes to the light. Then the light will show that the things he has done were done through God" (John 3:21).

MY PERSONAL THOUGHTS AND ACTION STEPS:

_____

_____

_____

_____

_____

_____

_____

_____

_____

_____

_____

_____

_____

_____

_____

_____

_____

_____

_____

32

DID I LEAVE MY VIRGINITY AT YOUR HOUSE?

L ast week Wendy's life was altered forever. She had sex for the first time. Wendy is no ordinary high school student; she's a strong Christian leader in our church. She's influential on her campus, respected by her peers, and popular in the youth group.

She had been infatuated with Tom for several months. One night while Tom's parents were out, Tom and Wendy were listening to music in his room. Relaxation and laughter led to kissing, which soon flared into passionate lust and moved them to the bed. Within minutes Wendy was naked and Tom's sexual fantasy was fulfilled.

Wendy believed it was the passion of the moment which caused her to yield. She loved attention from Tom, and when they were alone that night she didn't think it could get any

Both Tom and Wendy felt soiled with guilt.

better. Tom, on the other hand, was performing out of his lust. He made no secret of the fact that his interest in Wendy did not extend beyond a one-night fling. He told me later, "What's the big deal? I wanted sex and she was willing."

After their brief sexual experience, both Tom and Wendy felt soiled with guilt. Wendy's guilt was from yielding to Tom sexually, while Tom's guilt was from knowing he had violated Wendy. In trying to cover his guilt, Tom directed his anger at Wendy for "seducing him."

When Wendy shared her story with me, tears rolled down her face. She was obviously destroyed with shame. She knew her actions weren't right. "And it wasn't even enjoyable," she sobbed. "The kissing was great, but the sex hurt. I was scared. He was in a hurry and I hated it. He was selfish and I was dumb. It wasn't anything like the movies."

Sure, it's easy to sit back and call Tom a jerk. But what is Wendy going to do now? She's depressed and feels used, abused, and broken. It's during these times when the words of Jesus feel so comforting to those who hurt from sexual sin. An angry crowd wanted to kill the woman caught in adultery, but Jesus saw her brokenness, and He offered her forgiveness and encouraged her to start over again.

God designed sex for marriage; that's how it works best. But if you lose your virginity before marriage, Christ's message hasn't changed. He says to those who seek forgiveness and healing for sexual sin, "I accept you, I forgive you, I love you and I want to help you move on."

Something to think about:

"Jesus was left there alone with the woman [caught in adultery]. She was standing before him. Jesus stood up again and asked her, 'Woman, all of those people have gone. Has no one judged you guilty?' She answered, 'No one has judged me, sir.' Then Jesus said, 'So I also don't judge you. You may go now, but don't sin again' " (John 8:9-11).

MY PERSONAL THOUGHTS AND ACTION STEPS:	

33

CAN I STILL BE JOYFUL WHEN I'M NOT HAPPY?

It's no secret that we Christians desire to be happy, fulfilled, and joyful people. When things are going well, life is good. People ask, "How's it going?" and we respond by saying, "Very well! Thanks for asking." It's great when we can answer this way honestly. But what about the times when things aren't going so well, when circumstances enter our lives and rob us of our joy?

Eddie accepted Christ into his life at camp and he became a different person. He couldn't believe the new joy he discovered as a result of his commitment. People were warm and accepting toward him, and he began to see others in a different light.

Everything was great until he got back to school. During track practice Eddie messed up his hand-off on the relay and his teammates hassled him for

> *Joy is different from happiness.*

his mistake. Eddie blew up and left practice cussing at everyone. He talked to me about two weeks later, explaining that he had lost his new joy because he cussed out his friends. He even wondered if he was still a Christian.

I tried to explain to Eddie that Christian joy is a unique gift from God. Joy is different from happiness. Happiness is closely related to the word *happening*, which suggests that happiness is based on something happening to us. Happiness is circumstantial. If I get a new car, I'm happy. If I get new clothes, I'm happy. If someone says something nice, I'm happy. There's nothing wrong with happiness, but it's based on circumstances which tend to shift. Happiness is the result of an action, and if that action doesn't happen, our happiness goes out the window. Eddie lost his happiness at track practice because of the circumstance of losing his temper. But joy is different. It's not based on a circumstance, happening, or action—positive or negative. Joy is an attitude. Eddie didn't lose his joy.

The Bible is not oblivious to difficult circumstances. It tells us that difficulty and joy are not mutually exclusive; rather, they are close friends. The apostle James revealed this by encouraging Christians to be joyful when (notice that it's *when*, not *if*) they encounter problems (see James 1:2). And Jesus said that His followers would go through difficult times

Joy is always available. It's an attitude we develop.

in the world. But He commanded us to be cheerful in them because He has overcome the world (see John 16:33).

Pain is unavoidable, and being happy is conditional. But joy is always available. It's an attitude we develop as we become dependent on God. We will go through difficult times (that's what this book is all about!), but we can remain joyful in spite of negative circumstances. Our happiness will shift depending on circumstances, but not our joy. Joy is a gift of the Spirit that will lift us above our circumstances.

Something to think about:

"Be full of joy in the Lord always. I will say again, be full of joy" (Philippians 4:4).

MY PERSONAL THOUGHTS AND ACTION STEPS:

_____

_____

_____

_____

_____

_____

_____

_____

_____

_____

_____

_____

_____

_____

_____

_____

_____

_____

_____

_____

_____

34

ARE MONEY AND HAPPINESS RELATED?

Our church is surrounded by wealthy communities. Several years ago I was involved with the Williamses, a wealthy family interested in our youth ministry. They lived in a three-million-dollar mansion. Their monthly house payments were greater than my annual salary. Each of the Williams kids had a huge room, and they all had televisions, computers, and video games. The house was packed with expensive possessions and frivolous extras. After visiting, I would leave in amazement, hoping some day that I'd be rich. I used to think it would be great to have enough money to do whatever I wanted.

But during the year the Williamses were involved in our ministry, I watched their family suffer from problem after problem, and eventually fall apart. These weren't minor problems, but biggies—rebellion, drugs, marital unfaithfulness, divorce, and suicide. I learned from this family that money can buy toys, but it can't buy happiness.

My friend Barry, a junior in high school, lives in a huge house in the hills near our church. When I go to his house, I can't believe how beautiful it is. When Barry's friends come over, they talk about how rich his dad is

I learned from this family that money can buy toys, but it can't buy happiness.

and how lucky—and spoiled—Barry is. But when I asked Barry about the happiest time in his life, he told me it was when he lived in a small, one-story house. His family was still together then. He remembers the whole family eating together, playing with his dad in the front yard, and going on family vacations. Barry lives in a bigger home now, but he also has two sets of parents who live miles from one another. Barry is content, but he was happiest when his family was together. He has learned the same lesson that I learned from the Williamses: Money can't buy happiness.

Many wealthy people don't see themselves as being special, and they often wish they didn't have the problems and responsibilities that go along with wealth. Some people don't feel the need for big bucks, while others dream and fantasize about wealth. Those who strive to have it all often lose their sense of priority about what's really important. They work hard to gain their fortune, but once they get it, they often lose that which was really important.

My hope is that you can join Barry and me in learning that money alone can't buy happiness. If you happen to have a lot of money, learn to use your money in ways that please God. If you don't have much money, consider yourself wealthy because only true happiness will make you rich.

Something to think about:

"The love of money causes all kinds of evil. Some people have left the true faith because they want to get more and more money. But they have caused themselves much sorrow" (1 Timothy 6:10); "Love the Lord your God with all your heart, soul and mind" (Matthew 22:37).

MY PERSONAL THOUGHTS AND ACTION STEPS:

_____

_____

_____

_____

_____

_____

_____

_____

_____

_____

_____

_____

_____

_____

_____

_____

35

MOODINESS PLUS MANIPULATION EQUALS A MESS

What do you think about when you hear the word moodiness? Do you think of silence? anger? unpredictability? depression? I bet you can name at least one moody person. They're everywhere; we are surrounded by them on a daily basis. And many of them are Christians.

Moodiness is an inward feeling which is communicated by an outward action. We get moody when things don't go right, and we want other people to know that we are mad or frustrated at a particular individual or situation. We express our moodiness to gain attention. We know that moodiness affects others, and we want others to be affected so we will gain their compassion. Through compassion we get the attention and acceptance we want. Basically, we use others to bring us out of our moodiness. This is both unfair and selfish.

Those of us who are moody need to learn to deal with our problems, and not get moody

When moodiness rules, you tend to manipulate those around you.

over them, so that helpless individuals aren't abused. If others are needed to solve a problem, we should bring them in on a friendship or consultation basis. If we ask others to *help* us with our problems, we won't manipulate them to *feel guilty* for our problems.

117

The people in your life are precious assets. They are God's gifts to you. When moodiness rules, you tend to manipulate those around you and treat them as objects for selfish gain. If you can remember that moodiness leads to selfish and immature acts, you may be less likely to let your moodiness affect others.

Something to think about:

"My brothers, God called you to be free. But do not use your freedom as an excuse to do the things that please your sinful self. Serve each other with love" (Galatians 5:13).

MY PERSONAL THOUGHTS AND ACTION STEPS:

36

PEOPLE ARE OUT OF CONTROL

Once we arranged with a carpet company to lay new carpet in our house while we were gone on vacation. When we returned our house was a mess. There were carpet scraps all over the place, smears of brown glue on the wall, and cigarette burns on our table. We were very frustrated because our expectations were shattered. We were hoping to come home to a great-looking house, and instead it looked worse than when we left. We had no control over the people who were supposed to do the job, and they let us down.

Steve is one of my favorite high school students. I had spent a lot of time with him, hoping to help him mature in his relationship with Christ. One night Steve showed up at a church activity drunk. I couldn't believe it. Was I wasting my time? Did Steve let me down? Or did he just blow it?

We can't force anyone to live up to our expectations.

I've learned by working with people that we can't force anyone to live up to our expectations. People move, think, and breathe according to their own individual agendas. When we place expectations on them, we attempt to force them into boxes we've created to meet our needs. And it never works.

If you think that any one person—parent, boyfriend, teacher, youth pastor, or friend—can be your total source of joy, you will be let down. When you place your expectations for joy on a person or on people in general, you will always be let down.

Our God is a jealous god. God has made it clear that He will not be one of many gods in our lives, nor will He accept anything less than first place. God's desire is that we make Him, and only Him, our source of joy. God is consistent; He's the only one who will never let you down.

Something to think about:

"Jesus answered, 'Love the Lord your God with all your heart, soul and mind' " (Matthew 22:37); "Then God spoke all these words: 'I am the Lord your God. I brought you out of the land of Egypt where you were slaves. You must not have any other gods except me' " (Exodus 20:1-3).

MY PERSONAL THOUGHTS AND ACTION STEPS:	_____

PEPSI, POPCORN & PORNOGRAPHY: WHAT'S THE BIG DEAL?

I t was midnight and I was sitting in a booth of a 24-hour fast-food restaurant trying to get some writing done. Cathy was out of town and I wanted to write in a different atmosphere. The fast-food place just happened to have an all-you-can-drink Pepsi machine that kept me fueled for writing.

On one trip to the machine for another refill, I saw a guy in a booth staring at the pictures (I doubt that many guys read the articles) in a pornographic magazine. When I got back to my table, I began thinking about how pornography is a trap for millions of males (and females too, but to a lesser degree). It's the trap of sexual exploitation, a fascination with lewd photographs of naked, beautiful women. No matter what the telephone ads say, for many men, pornographic material is the next best thing to being there.

Most guys say, "What's the big deal about a few skin pictures? I'll never meet those girls anyway. Isn't it better to look at the pictures than to get in trouble with a live girl?" There's a dangerous dimension to pornography that isn't very obvious when we just look at the

> *There's a dangerous dimension to pornography that isn't very obvious when we just look at the pictures.*

121

pictures. The greatest danger is the unseen, that which takes place in the mind after the viewing pleasure is over. It's like a glass of Pepsi. I can't see the 12 tablespoons of sugar it contains, but it still affects my body. Or it's like filling my mouth with a handful of popcorn. I don't notice the unpopped kernel until I bite it. The unseen suddenly has a startling effect when I chomp down on it and crack a tooth.

When looking at the "harmless" pictures, we don't think about how those images shape our thinking and distort our view of women, sex, and reality. We fail to discern that pornography controls how we want the women in our lives (girlfriends, future wives, etc.) to look. We unconsciously place expectations upon women to look like beauty queens. I suspect that pornography plays a role in the rise of eating disorders among women today. Girls want to be thinner and prettier, often because guys are telling them that they are fat compared to the girls in their fantasy magazines.

> *If we only realized that pornography isn't reality.*

If we only realized that pornography isn't reality. We are allowing one dimension of a person that we will never meet affect how we think about and treat women. When I was a young boy, my dad told me that all women have the same body parts, but not all women have the same mind, thoughts, inner beauty, concern for others, family background, etc. He was encouraging me to be concerned about more than just a woman's body. There are many other dimensions of women that need to be appreciated.

Pretty girls aren't difficult to find; they're a dime a dozen. But one who has her act together is a great catch.

Something to think about:

"Charm can fool you, and beauty can trick you. But a woman who respects the Lord should be praised" (Proverbs 31:30).

MY PERSONAL THOUGHTS AND ACTION STEPS:

_____

_____

_____

_____

_____

_____

_____

_____

_____

_____

_____

_____

_____

_____

_____

_____

38

DID I SAY THAT?

I had just finished playing a pick-up basketball game with a group of high school students. I concluded from the content of their language that these guys weren't Christians (even though they said God and Jesus a lot). Missed shots and bad passes were followed by four-letter words. By the tone of their voices it seemed as though their anger was therapeutic. I quickly tired of listening to these guys during the game, and I found myself getting angry just being around them. I kept thinking about how stupid they sounded. I know cussing is a problem for some students. Because verbal obscenities are so universally accepted today, many people aren't even conscious of the words they use. Profanity has become a customary part of daily language in our culture. An objective opinion would view profanity as a bad habit which is rude and unpleasant. The

Language is a result of the heart's content.

more habitual it becomes, the harder it is to stop.

Geoff was an exception at our basketball game. After the game I asked him if he was friends with the other guys. His head hung in embarrassment as he nodded yes. I responded by telling him that I respected his good attitude and language, and that he stood out positively among his friends. He said he was a Christian striving for purity in his lifestyle. He stopped cussing by simply listening to his friends.

"Their language sounded so funny and immature to me," Geoff said. "It came to the point where I began to laugh at the way they talked. My friends notice that I don't cuss. One guy told me that he could never stop cussing, and I laughed again. Cussing makes people sound so dumb."

Christ tells us to evaluate our language by looking at our hearts. If language is a result of the heart's content (and Jesus said it is), we need to keep a continual check on what we're putting inside our hearts. If you want to change your language, realize that it will take time. You will screw up for awhile. Though it's a tough habit to break, profanity can be broken. Remember that we consciously choose every word that we speak, so we are totally in control of what we say. Choose your words carefully and you'll quickly notice a difference. Others will too.

Something to think about:

"If you want good fruit, you must make the tree good. If your tree is not good, then it will have bad fruit. A tree is known by the kind of fruit it produces. You snakes! You are evil people! How can you say anything good? The mouth speaks the things that are in the heart. A good person has good things in his heart. And so he speaks the good things that come from his heart. But an evil person has evil in his heart. So he speaks the evil things that come from his heart" (Matthew 12:33-35).

MY PERSONAL THOUGHTS AND ACTION STEPS:

39

PUMPING UP YOUR INSIDES

Recently I watched the bodybuilding championships on television. There seem to be two extreme opinions about this sport. Some people think those muscle-bound bodies are repulsive, while other people view them as works of art. Regardless of your opinion, you must appreciate the amount of time these men and women devote to their bodies in order to develop the greatest potential for their muscles. They spend hours pumping iron in hopes that their muscles will enlarge. And by paying close attention to what they eat and drink, bodybuilders can mold their bodies to a precise weight and shape. Then in competition they flex their muscles to display the results of their demanding training. The amount of time and energy bodybuilders devote to the human body is remarkable. As I watched the program, I wondered what would happen if we Christians gave the same amount of attention to our

I wondered what would happen if we Christians gave the same amount of attention to our inner beings.

inner beings. What kind of people would we be if we devoted ourselves to spirit-building like a bodybuilder devotes himself or herself to bodybuilding? Developing inner maturity demands many of the same disciplines which bodybuilders employ.

127

The greatest obstacle to our spiritual development is our lack of discipline. Praying every day is strenuous spiritual exercise. Being in continual fellowship with God is demanding on our time. And reading the Bible on a regular basis sometimes seems like a nearly unachievable feat.

Spirit-building is often difficult for us because the internal rewards are not as spectacular to us as the external rewards of bodybuilding. I can go to the garage, clutch a barbell, and do curls for 15 minutes, and I will see immediate results. Blood will surge into my muscles and enlarge my biceps. But the rewards we get from prayer and Bible reading are internal—personal and spiritual maturity. And these rewards don't seem as gratifying to us as large muscles. Sometimes I wish that God would make me look stronger when I'm spiritually disciplined so I can better appreciate my efforts.

Being spiritually disciplined is difficult. It begins by deciding that internal growth is worth taking the necessary time and effort to pursue. We all struggle with consistency in spiritual discipline, but keep pressing on. Intimacy with God is a great reward.

Something to think about:

"Training your body helps you in some ways, but serving God helps you in every way. Serving God brings you blessings in this life and in the future life, too" (1 Timothy 4:8).

MY PERSONAL THOUGHTS AND ACTION STEPS:

_____

_____

_____

_____

_____

_____

_____

_____

_____

_____

_____

_____

_____

_____

_____

_____

40

DEDICATED TO DEDICATION & HARD WORK

Cindy was an active member of our church youth group. She made a commitment to Christ as a freshman and lived as though her faith was an important part of her life. Everything seemed great until her junior year. Then disillusionment attacked her faith and Cindy began hanging out with the party crowd. Drinking, parties, and guys became her passion; she lived for the weekend.

Cindy's generous parents gave her everything she wanted. She attended college to please her parents and to keep from going to work. Her first job was with her dad's company four years after graduating from high school. But as Cindy got older, her desire for guys, parties, and the easy life increased. When she was 21, she married Craig, a wealthy real estate investor. Those of us who watched from afar thought Cindy had it made.

She made all her own choices. Now she has to live with the consequences.

Since she didn't need to work, she spent her days driving her Mercedes, shopping, socializing, and playing tennis. Many of her friends envied Cindy's apparently perfect life.

Within a year of her wedding, Cindy's life radically changed when Craig moved to New York with another woman. When the gossip hit the streets, Cindy's friends were moved from envy to empathy. They couldn't help hurting for Cindy, whose life was shattered. Now at 23, Cindy lives with her parents and works for her dad.

When you read Cindy's tragic story, who is the first person you want to blame? Cindy's husband? He's the one who pulled the plug and skipped town. He's an easy target. Cindy's parents? Could they have been too supportive? Maybe they should have made her work at an earlier age and should not have supplied her with everything she wanted. But what about Cindy? She made all her own choices. Now she has to live with the consequences. The thing that bothers me most about this story is that it's true. This kind of thing happens every day.

Cindy's story is a lesson in something called reality. Cindy wasn't naive, but she may have deluded herself into thinking that the world was going to take care of her so she didn't have to work.

> *Cindy's story is a lesson in something called reality.*

That's not the real world; that's a fantasy. It may sound cruel, but the world doesn't owe Cindy—or any of us—anything. Life doesn't just fall into your lap. Making it in life requires that you work for what you need and want. It's your responsibility to work to make things happen. You can't rely on somebody else's dedication.

The same truth applies in your relationship with God. It won't just happen; that's a fantasy. It takes dedication and hard work; that's reality. Sure, it's tough to work diligently in order to grow closer to a God you can't even see. But no one can grow for you; your personal faith is your responsibility.

Something to think about:

"No one has seen God, but Jesus is exactly like him. Christ ranks higher than all the things that have been made" (Colossians 1:15).

MY PERSONAL THOUGHTS AND ACTION STEPS:

_____

_____

_____

_____

_____

_____

_____

_____

_____

_____

_____

_____

_____

_____

_____

_____

_____

41

WHAT'S SO WRONG WITH SEX THAT MAKES IT SO DUMB?

Sex seems so confusing to teenagers. Is everyone in your school or youth group doing it? Some say yes with a rousing cheer, while others express an apprehensive no. I know this is a major struggle for students today. Don't you wish someone would just make it black-and-white so it wouldn't be such a battle?

I have little doubt that you know what's right and wrong when it comes to sexual decisions. But do you know what's smart? When it comes to sex, I try to encourage people to think long-term. What's going to be smart ten years from now about the sexual decision you make today? Wendy, whom you read about earlier, knew it wasn't right to have sex with Tom, but she didn't realize how dumb it was. She was dumb not to think about the implications of wrong behavior on her future life. What would have happened if she became pregnant? How will her sexual

> *When it comes to sex, I try to encourage people to think long-term.*

misconduct affect her when she meets her future husband? How will she answer her children when they ask her about sex? Her decision to yield during a passionate moment was as dumb as it was wrong.

I'm not trying to let Tom off the hook; his approach to sex was dumb too. He also needed to think about how his

133

sexual decisions were going to affect him in the long run. What if Wendy became pregnant? Could he still fulfill his dreams for college? I know of so many kids who get caught in the backseat of the car or in an empty house without thinking through the long-term effects of their wrong sexual decisions.

I don't need to waste my time telling you what's right and what's wrong about sex; you already know. But what's smart? How different is your life going to be as a result of the sexual decisions you make? Thinking about the smart questions is what's right. Be smart!

Something to think about:

"God wants you to be holy and to stay away from sexual sins. He wants each one of you to learn how to take a wife in a way that is holy and honorable. Don't use your body for sexual sin. The people who do not know God use their bodies for that" (1 Thessalonians 4:3-5).

MY
PERSONAL
THOUGHTS
AND
ACTION
STEPS:

_____

_____

_____

_____

_____

_____

_____

_____

_____

_____

_____

_____

_____

_____

_____

_____

MAKING SCHOOL COUNT, EVEN WHEN YOU THINK IT'S A PRISON

42

I know very few students who have a passionate love for school. Some kids I know think school is okay, and others, like Lisa, think school is a prison. Lisa is an intelligent Christian girl with a lot going for her, but she's just one of those kids who hates school. She loves seeing her friends and she enjoys the social aspects, but she hates having to be there five days a week "for a million years." She has considered dropping out several times.

Lisa and I have spent time together trying to figure out a way to change her attitude toward school. Every time we talk she refers to school as a prison. I wanted to take her to a prison to show her the difference, but her parents wouldn't let me, so we had to figure out another way.

As we began to search the Scriptures for some answers, we came across the writings of Paul. Paul spent a lot of time in prison. As we read Philippians, one of the letters Paul wrote from prison, we discovered it to be a letter of joy. Paul was joyful because of the way God used him in prison. He wrote that what happened to him there served to spread the news of Jesus. How did this happen? It was

> *Lives have been changed as a result of others serving time "behind bars."*

probably the combined result of his attitude, his lifestyle, and his message while in prison. He explained that some prisoners became Christians and some Christians became bolder and more courageous in their faith as a result of his time in prison.

I asked Lisa several questions to help her see that her time in school could be like Paul's time in prison: "What message are you bringing to your school? What are other students learning about God as a result of your lifestyle, actions, and message? Are other Christians living differently as a result of your encouragement to them?" These are tough questions.

What about you? Maybe you should ask yourself these questions if you really want to make a difference at your school as a Christian. Allow Paul's example to be your goal in making your time in school count. There's a lot more than formal education happening at your school. You have an opportunity to make a tremendous impact on your peers, who are at a prime age to make decisions for Christ.

If you're tempted to call your school a prison, do it, but remember that lives have been changed as a result of others serving time "behind bars." Who's going to be different as a result of your prison sentence?

Something to think about:

"Brothers, I want you to know that what has happened to me has helped to spread the Good News. I am in prison because I am a believer in Christ. All the palace guards and everyone else knows this. I am still in prison, but most of the believers feel better about it now. And so they are much braver about telling the Good News about Christ" (Philippians 1:12-14).

MY PERSONAL THOUGHTS AND ACTION STEPS:

_____
_____
_____
_____
_____
_____
_____
_____
_____
_____
_____
_____
_____
_____

FOR GIRLS ONLY: IS SEX THE ONLY THING GUYS THINK ABOUT?

Most of the guys I talk to do more thinking from below their waists than from above their necks. If guys thought about their schoolwork as often as they think about sex, they'd never have any homework. Guys think about sex, dream about sex, and talk about sex. They do more talking than acting (which is good), but with all their talking, they build up a great degree of desire for sex. They want it!

As in the story of Tom and Wendy earlier in the book, a lot of guys only view girls as a means for fulfilling their sexual goals. Girls often walk blindly into the trap looking for a meaningful relationship. A girl wants a guy who is gentle, tender, loving, strong, and affirming—someone who is going to treat her nicely and make her feel good about herself. But a guy is looking for someone who is cute, fun, and sexually willing. Can you see what's going to happen? You probably already know because you see it happen every day.

The other girls were amazed at what they were hearing.

Like Tom, a guy will do everything he can to *appear* gentle, respectful, and kind, hoping the girl will be *emotionally* turned on. And inside she's saying, "This is great!" In the meantime, the guy is *physically* turned on and his insides are saying, "This is great, I can't wait, let's mate!" Wendy's sad first experience with sex isn't unusual.

During college, I took a class in human sexuality. When the professor told the class exactly how guys think, the guys in the class began to slip under their chairs in embarrassment. The "experienced" girls in class were nodding their heads in agreement, while the other girls were amazed at what they were hearing. Girls need to understand the way guys think, whether it's right or wrong. When my wife and I present sex seminars for the girls in our church, I try to tell them how guys think. Some don't believe me and think I'm a pervert for making such statements. Unfortunately, many learn too late that I'm right.

So should girls spend the rest of their lives thinking that guys are the scum of the earth? I don't think so. I don't write this so that girls will stay away from guys. I just want you to be educated on how they think. It's probably not medically correct to say that guys' thoughts are controlled by their hormones, but their actions often validate that claim.

Girls, please realize that guys have a much easier time controlling themselves when you let them know your boundaries right from the beginning. When you do this, you take away the mystery and they don't have to experiment on you to see how far you'll go. Understand that many guys will go as far as you let them. If your guy loses interest in you because of where you draw the line, he's not a guy that would care for you after he got what he wanted.

Something to think about:

"But clothe yourselves with the Lord Jesus Christ. Forget about satisfying your sinful self" (Romans 13:14).

MY PERSONAL THOUGHTS AND ACTION STEPS:

_____

_____

_____

_____

_____

_____

_____

_____

_____

_____

_____

_____

_____

_____

_____

_____

_____

_____

_____

44

YOUR PARENTS AND YOUR STRUGGLE FOR FREEDOM

Your parents love you. But that doesn't mean you will always get along with them, especially at your age. There seems to be something built into adolescents that makes them want to argue or be defensive when communicating with parents. You're in the process of securing your independence, but you're still in a dependent situation while living with your parents. Your heart wants to be free. You want to set your own curfew, go out with your own friends, and run your life without having to answer all your parents' questions. But you're still not free. This is a common struggle.

Take Gavin, for example. Gavin is 16 and he desires complete freedom with the family car. He wants to stay out late with his friends, and he gets mad when his parents want to know where he's going and when he'll be back. He has slacked off on his homework and his grades have dropped to an undesirable level. His parents finally put some restrictions on him and limited his freedom. Gavin went crazy and stopped talking to them.

> *When he grows to be independent from his parents, he still needs to respect them.*

Gavin needs to realize that as long as he is *dependent* on his parents for food, shelter, etc., he needs to honor them. And when he grows to be independent from his parents, he still needs to respect them. In my own life, for example, if my parents didn't want me to buy a house, I would respect their opinion, but I wouldn't have to honor them by not buying a house. My independence allows me freedom from their control, but I still have a biblical command to respect my parents.

Until you become independent from your parents, realize that they are real people. They have struggles and hurts just like you do. They are not perfect—as you well know. But they are your parents, and they are trying to nurture your move towards independence. Parenting is a tough and frightening job, and that's why some of their decisions are hasty or wrong. Forgive them and honor them anyway.

When Jay was in my high school group, he had a hard time with his parents. From his perspective, home life was terrible and every minute communicating with his parents was painful. I told him that when he graduated from high school and moved away, his love for his parents would increase. A couple of years later he thought I was a prophet,

Parenting is a tough and frightening job, and that's why some of their decisions are hasty or wrong.

because that's exactly what happened. When Jay came back to town after being away, he said, "Doug, you were right. I've really learned to love and respect my parents."

Things changed when Jay moved from dependence to independence. Your situation may also change, but you don't have to wait that long to love, respect, and honor your parents. There is hope for you and your parents while you are still dependent. Keep trying!

Something to think about:

"Honor your father and your mother. Then you will live a long time in the land. The Lord your God is going to give you this land" (Exodus 20:12).

MY PERSONAL THOUGHTS AND ACTION STEPS:

_____
_____
_____
_____
_____
_____
_____
_____
_____
_____
_____
_____
_____
_____
_____
_____
_____
_____

45

WHAT'S SO GREAT ABOUT NOT MAKING THE TEAM?

When this book was in its beginning stages, one of the topics I wanted to write about was the disappointment of not making the team. I felt this was an important topic for students because it happens on a daily basis, and the negative feelings which accompany rejection are powerful. But it had been many years since I played a sport for which I had to try out and be selected in order to participate. So I decided to cross the topic off my list because I couldn't recall my firsthand feelings for this experience. But that all changed recently when Cathy and I went on vacation. This story proves that God has a great sense of humor.

We were at a resort filled with hundreds of people and more activities than we could possibly participate in. As I looked over the week's program, I noticed a softball game scheduled for Wednesday afternoon. I quickly signed up for the game, anticipating the fun of playing my favorite sport.

> *There is no consolation for not making the team. You feel rejected, isolated, and lonely.*

Prior to Wednesday's game, Cathy and I participated in some of the other activities—ping-pong, water volleyball, sailing, water polo. I had fun, but I couldn't wait for Wednesday to come so I could break loose on the softball field. Wednesday finally arrived, and I went to the field and started warming up with the other guys. But before long over 40 guys had shown up, and we only needed 20 for the game. Two captains were appointed and they each selected nine players. As you probably guessed, I was not chosen to play. I couldn't believe it. Why did they overlook me? I can play softball. Maybe they judged my softball ability by the way I played ping-pong. I stink at ping-pong. Regardless of how they chose the teams, I wasn't on one.

All these crazy thoughts ran through my mind: *I'll sneak onto a team; I'll pray that someone gets hurt so I can replace him; I'll ask for my money back; I'll steal the ball and throw it in the ocean.* My feelings were hurt and I was thinking like a child. I didn't want to stick around and watch them play without me. I wanted to take my toys and go home.

There is no consolation for not making the team. You feel rejected, isolated, and lonely. You practiced so hard, and now you feel like a failure. And those who made the team don't stop playing and run over to ask how you're feeling. They begin the game without you no matter how you feel.

The only thing that can soothe the pain is the understanding that God has different standards for measuring us. God doesn't love us based on our ability to hit a softball, do the splits in cheer-

God has different standards for measuring us.

leading, make the weight in wrestling, sing in the choir, act in the play, or get chosen for the homecoming court. God looks at our hearts.

During the 1988 Olympics, I was very impressed by the attitudes of the American athletes. The reporters would ask, "How do you feel about losing the race and not winning a medal?" Several athletes responded by saying something like, "I came to Seoul to do my best. If I had won a medal, I would have been very pleased. But my greatest satisfaction comes from knowing that I did my best."

This is a winning attitude! Life is not intended to be a spectator sport. When it comes to making the team, do your best and run to win, then rest in the satisfaction of knowing that you did the best you could do. And in the process, remember that you have already been chosen by the greatest Captain of all time.

Something to think about:

"Brothers, I know that I have not yet reached that goal. But there is one thing I always do: I forget the things that are past. I try as hard as I can to reach the goal that is before me. I keep trying to reach the goal and get the prize. That prize is mine because God called me through Christ to the life above" (Philippians 3:13-14).

MY PERSONAL THOUGHTS AND ACTION STEPS:	

46

LIFE CAN BE RISKY BUSINESS

Taking risks is frightening. We are often afraid to risk because we fear the unknown. We don't know if our risk is going to meet with success or failure. No one likes to fail because failure makes us feel inadequate and look stupid, and our confidence is weakened. The fear of risking results in people only doing the things in which they know they can succeed to a large degree. They would rather not risk than to risk and fail, therefore depriving themselves of some adventure in life because they are afraid they will look stupid.

With the possibility of failure waiting around every corner, it's no wonder that so many of us are afraid to risk. We carefully evaluate the potential outcome of a risk to decide if it's worth taking. If we feel the reward is great enough, we may take the risk. If the reward is insignificant in comparison to the potential failure, we won't take the chance.

All of us have heard of individuals whose lives have been prematurely snuffed out by accident or illness. People write books and spend count-

Since life is so precious and so short, how can we waste the time we have by living boring, riskless lives?

less hours discussing the reasons for untimely deaths. The answers to these tough questions are beyond me. But my question is: Since life is so precious and so short, how can we waste the time we have by living boring, riskless lives?

If we don't take some risks in life, we may never find out who we are and what we can do. We may never discover our gifts and, therefore, never find out how God can use us. God gave us this incredible playground called earth to enjoy and explore. Our failure to risk limits our ability to be the people God wants us to be on this playground. God doesn't desire for us to fail; He desires for us to live. And in order to experience life at its fullest, we've got to be willing to risk.

The following poem was written anonymously by a man late in his life. He seems to be explaining his regret for not risking in life:

> If I had my life to live over again, I'd try to make more mistakes next time.
> I would relax, I would limber up, I would be sillier than I have been this trip.
> I know of very few things I would take seriously.
> I would take more trips. I would be crazier.
> I would climb more mountains, swim more rivers, and watch more sunsets.
> I would do more walking and looking.
> I would eat more ice cream and less beans.
> I would have more actual troubles, and fewer imaginary ones.
> You see, I'm one of those people who lives life prophylactically and sensibly hour after hour, day after day. I've been one of those people who never go anywhere without a thermometer, a hot-water bottle, a gargle, a raincoat, aspirin, and a parachute.

If I had to do it over again I would go places, do things, and travel lighter than I have.

If I had my life to live over I would start barefooted earlier in the spring and stay that way later in the fall.

I would play hooky more.

I wouldn't make such good grades, except by accident.

I would ride on more merry-go-rounds.

I'd pick more daisies.

Something to think about:

"I can do all things through Christ because he gives me strength" (Philippians 4:13).

MY PERSONAL THOUGHTS AND ACTION STEPS:	_____

47

DOES EVERYONE GO THROUGH TRANSITIONS?

"**M**y parents don't understand me. They tell me that they went through tough times when they were my age, but they must not remember them."

"I don't know what I think about God. How can I think about Him when I don't even know who I am?"

"Sometimes I think evil and dirty thoughts, and that makes me feel guilty. I hope I don't feel this way for the rest of my life."

"Yesterday I had to go up to the front of the class, and I know that everyone was laughing at my looks. I felt so stupid."

These statements represent the thoughts and fears my students regularly tell me about. I'm sure they're similar to some of yours. These thoughts reflect the period of transition you are in right now. During this youthful transition called adolescence, you act in different ways, your moods swing, your friends change, and you no longer accept "because I told you so" for an answer. You second-guess the values and

Adolescence is a stage, a transition into adulthood.

morals you were raised on because you are trying to figure out if you believe everything you were taught. A recurring question arises in your thoughts: "Who am I anyway?"

You like the sound of the cliché: "There's light at the end of the tunnel." It encourages you that, as soon as you graduate, life will be so much easier. You'll be 18 then, your parents can't tell you what to do anymore, and you won't have mandatory homework. But, unfortunately, that rumor is a lie. Life doesn't get easier after the transition.

Don't get me wrong. I'm not saying that the adolescent transition is easy. You couldn't pay me enough money to be a teenager again. I hated zits, the pressure to date, trying to be in the right crowd, and the battleground at home. I get sick just thinking about going through it again.

Adolescence is a stage, a transition into adulthood. You'll have several more transitions during your lifetime. The coping skills you develop and use during the adolescent transition will again be used in future times of transition.

In order to help you survive this transition and prepare you for the next, you should constantly work at being the best teenager you can be. It's in this pursuit that you will develop qualities which will serve you the rest of

Constantly work at being the best teenager you can be.

your life. Remember that you're no different from anyone else, because everyone goes through adolescence. What separates quality people from average people is how they handle this vital transition. Don't forget: God is on your side.

Something to think about:

"I pray that Christ will live in your hearts because of your faith. I pray that your life will be strong in love and be built on love. And I pray that you and all God's holy people will have the power to understand the greatness of Christ's love. I pray that you can understand how wide and how long and how high and how deep that love is. Christ's love is greater than any person can ever know. But I pray that you will be able to know that love. Then you can be filled with the fullness of God" (Ephesians 3:17-19).

MY PERSONAL THOUGHTS AND ACTION STEPS:

_____

_____

_____

_____

_____

_____

_____

_____

_____

_____

_____

_____

48

WHEN IS IT CLEAR TO BE TRANSPARENT?

Not too long ago I spent some time goofing around with Rand and Greg, two unique and special friends of mine who had just finished their first year of college. It was great to see them. They had been in my high school youth group for four years. We shared a lot of crazy times together—fun, wild, intense, and personal.

It's always been important to me that these guys see me as I really am, and not as the youth pastor who has it all together, because I don't have it all together. One time Rand and Greg broke into my garage and rearranged everything. They thought I'd come home and say, "Hey, this is great! What a clever prank! I can't wait to spend the next four hours cleaning up this mess."

Instead, they saw my anger and frustration. I wanted them to understand the difference between a humorous prank and a destructive prank. This was definitely the latter, and they knew so by my response. We wound up having a good time cleaning up the mess, but they saw a different side to Doug Fields. I wasn't the same Doug Fields that day who greets them with a Sunday morning smile. Throughout their years in high school, we continued to become good friends as a result of being ourselves with each other.

> *Being transparent means letting another person know who you really are.*

The incident in my garage illustrates a powerful quality which can pull friends together and provide an atmosphere of healing in their relationships. It's called transparency. Being transparent means opening up to another person and letting him or her know who you really are. Transparency is frightening for many of us because we are afraid that we won't be accepted for who we are. We fear that we will be laughed at or that we will be rejected. So instead of being transparent we often put on masks so people will *not* know who we really are. We wear these masks like shields in our relationships to keep ourselves from getting hurt. At the same time, there's another side of us which desperately wants to tell others who we really are and let them see the real us.

Transparency will strengthen your friendships because you are allowing someone else to know you in an intimate way. By sharing your dreams, fantasies, struggles, fears, and doubts with another person, your hearts and lives will begin to bond together. My healthiest relationships are the ones where we have experienced transparency. In those relationships I'm able to express my feelings about anything and everything. And I know that no matter what I say or do, I will be loved and accepted by these friends.

> *There's another side of us which desperately wants to tell others who we really are and let them see the real us.*

In James 5:16 we are invited to admit our faults to one another and pray for one another so that we may be healed. Transparency allows us the freedom to list our weaknesses before another person. And, according to James 5:16, the result is healing. When we reveal areas in our lives in which we need help, we are opening those areas up for healing. The act of confessing our weaknesses to another person (in addition to God, who alone can forgive us) helps us get these feelings out in the open where they can be seen in a different light and from a new perspective. And this openness with each other makes us accountable to each other and motivates us to take action in resolving our sins.

Being transparent with someone can be a very rewarding experience. There's an indescribable feeling which comes from giving yourself to another person, being accepted by him, and opening up to him as he gives himself to you in return. Transparency is a powerful step in the direction of strong relationships. Be selective, begin slowly, and challenge each other to strive for the same level of transparency. You will be much more willing to risk letting another person know you if that person is also risking himself for you.

Something to think about:

"Do all these things; but most important, love each other. Love is what holds you all together in perfect unity. Let the peace that Christ gives control your thinking. You were all called together in one body to have peace. Always be thankful. Let the teaching of Christ live in you richly. Use all wisdom to teach and strengthen each other. Sing psalms, hymns, and spiritual songs with thankfulness in your hearts to God" (Colossians 3:14-16).

MY PERSONAL THOUGHTS AND ACTION STEPS:

_____

_____

_____

_____

_____

_____

_____

_____

_____

_____

_____

_____

_____

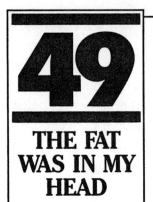

49

THE FAT WAS IN MY HEAD

Being overweight is tough! I know. Though I've never been obese, there was a period of my life when I was chubby and uncomfortable with how I looked and felt.

Growing up I was active in sports and never had to think about my weight. My metabolism was so rapid that I struggled to gain weight when I played football. I never had to watch what I ate, so I ate everything I wanted. But when I reached my 20s something changed and I started gaining weight. I continued to eat whatever I wanted, thinking I could run off the fattening calories. It sounded good, but it didn't work. The running helped me get in shape, but I didn't lose weight. My cardiovascular system was good, but my "love-handles" still bounced.

I allowed my body to get out of control, and my lifestyle was affected. Instead of swimming with my youth group, I just sat beside the pool with a towel wrapped around my waist. I

*(1) avoid fatty foods &
(2) burn up the fat in your system through regular exercise.*

strained to get into my pants. And my friends kept poking me in the stomach and saying, "Looks like you're picking up a few pounds." I was quickly motivated to change.

Everybody I talked to and every diet book I read promoted a different formula for losing weight. But all of

160

them agreed on two basic rules: (1) avoid fatty foods and (2) burn up the fat in your system through regular exercise. I sadly discovered that the foods I should avoid were the foods I loved: red meat, fried foods, avocados, butter, and, of course, any type of dessert. My discovery dropped me into depression and denial, and I tried to convince myself that I really didn't need to change my eating habits. Instead, I increased my exercise. But after a couple of months of strenuous exercise with no diet change, I still hadn't lost weight.

Finally, I admitted to myself that my undisciplined eating habits were the culprit, so I tried to stop eating fatty foods. To my surprise, I couldn't make myself stop eating the wrong foods. I had an eating problem. I'd do great for three days, then I'd go to a buffet and gorge myself until I was sick.

Eating right is a matter of lifestyle— learning to live without fat.

For the first time in my life I could relate to the smoker or drinker who was trying to quit. "Come on Fields, you wimp," I chided myself, riddled with guilt. "Why can't you stop eating?" I was hard on myself, but kept denying that it was a problem. I assured myself that I could quit if I really wanted to quit; I just didn't want it bad enough.

Finally, after admitting my problem and surrounding myself with people to hold me accountable for my eating, I started anew. Before I got serious about changing my eating habits, my body fat was 22 percent. After three months I tested at 14 percent, and three months later I tested at ten percent. I did it! I reduced the fat in my body.

161 ■

I learned a great deal about self-control, discipline, and accountability through my ordeal. I also learned that everyone is in control of his own eating habits and body size. Each of us holds the keys to how we look. I've never met anyone who is force-fed. We all feed ourselves, and we choose what—and how much—enters our mouths. Eating right is a matter of lifestyle—learning to live without fat. This lifestyle takes discipline and hard work. You may want to bring some people into your life who can hold you accountable for reaching your goals. But remember: You are ultimately in total control of what your body looks like. Good luck.

Something to think about:

"You should know that you yourselves are God's temple. God's Spirit lives in you.... God's temple is holy. You yourselves are God's temple" (1 Corinthians 3:16-17).

MY PERSONAL THOUGHTS AND ACTION STEPS:

_____

_____

_____

_____

_____

_____

_____

_____

_____

_____

_____

_____

_____

_____

_____

_____

_____

_____

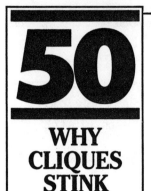

50

WHY CLIQUES STINK

Cliques are everywhere. They begin in preschool and continue into our adult society. Cliques surround us, frustrate us, and make our lives miserable. Actually they stink, and being involved in them makes us smell funny too. Unfortunately, cliques even exist in the church.

A clique can be defined as a group of people who aren't interested in including others into their group. You know what they're like; you've seen them in your neighborhood, church, school, and workplace. Cliques often form apart from conscious thought or action. A group of friends grows progressively tighter, and they are unaware that they exclude new members. Once you become aware that your group has become a clique, you need to respond by opening your group to accept others. This attitude of acceptance should be in response to your obedience and love for God.

Cliques also make youth groups look bad. In our youth group, if visitors aren't welcomed and included, they lose

> *The church should be the last place where people feel unwanted and unwelcomed.*

interest and leave, usually with bad feelings. Do visitors feel loved and accepted in your youth group? Your group may be filled with wonderful people, but if they're not friendly and accepting, visitors won't want to be around them.

Cliques can alienate people. You know how horrible it is to feel like you don't belong. Even when you know that God loves you unconditionally, you still have a hard time feeling good about yourself when you are excluded by a group. This is how people feel when you don't include them. It's especially sad that this type of alienation takes place in the church. The church should be the last place where people feel unwanted and unwelcomed.

Furthermore, cliques ruin God's plan for reaching other people. One of the ways in which God has chosen to reach non-believers is through His church. But when the church doesn't accept outsiders, it becomes a Christian club. If God wanted Christian clubs, He would have taken us to heaven right after we were saved so we would be with other Christians exclusively. Instead, God wants to use His church to reach others. We can't afford to have cliques in the church if we are to effectively live out God's plan for reaching others.

I suggest that you become a clique-buster. Start with one other person, and catch the vision together for breaking down cliques. Develop a strategy together that will educate others on the danger of cliques and on the action steps needed to reach the goal of accepting others. In the

> *When the church doesn't accept outsiders, it becomes a Christian club.*

meantime, become an example for your group. Begin reaching out in a loving manner to new people. Watch for them, greet them, and invite them to become part of your group. This doesn't mean that you must give up all your old friends, but that you allow new friends to join your old friends.

Ask God to give you and your group sensitivity. Before every program, meeting, or party ask God to make you sensitive to the needs of those you'll contact. God will direct you to those who feel uncomfortable. Every time you enter a situation where there are outsiders, put on your "glasses of sensitivity" by asking God to help you see where you can best be used.

Something to think about:

"This is my prayer for you: that your love will grow more and more; that you will have knowledge and understanding with your love; that you will see the difference between good and bad and choose the good; that you will be pure and without wrong for the coming of Christ" (Philippians 1:9-10).

MY PERSONAL THOUGHTS AND ACTION STEPS:

_____

_____

_____

_____

_____

_____

_____

_____

_____

51
DO YOU ALWAYS NEED TO WIN?

Professional athletes do their best to win. For them, winning is everything! The better they play, the more money they make. Though most of us don't have this type of performance anxiety, we still experience competitive pressure because we live in a world that acknowledges winners. We are always competing, whether we play the piano, paint, or play on the basketball team. We compete against ourselves, against a standard of excellence, and against others. Some people place such a big emphasis on winning that they will do whatever it takes to win. You hear about it in sports all the time. Cheating happens on the professional level and in colleges, high schools, and even little league teams.

These overly competitive attitudes are dangerous to Christian maturity. We must understand that winning isn't everything. The desire to win shouldn't cause us to compromise our integrity. It's fun to win, but the constant pressure to win can be destructive. This "always win" attitude sets us up for failure because we can't win at everything. It's impossible. There is always someone better.

> **"I was taught that a tie is a loss."**

Those who are willing to do anything to win have a competitive nature which is so intense that they hate to lose. Once I talked to a football player after a tie game who said, "I hate to lose." I quickly reminded him that

167

his team didn't lose; the final score was tied. But he replied, "I was taught that a tie *is* a loss." What a terrible attitude. Those who hate to lose are usually the "poor sports" who do the most complaining.

Intensely competitive people often base their self-images on whether they win or lose. (That's what I was like in high school.) They'll do anything to win, and when they lose, they aren't fun to be around. Their self-images rise and fall with their success or failure on the playing field. These people need help. Your friends who are the most competitive probably have the lowest self-images.

One of my strong desires is to help people develop an attitude of fun that isn't dependent on winning. You can be athletically uncoordinated, musically goofy, and academically stupid, and still have a winning attitude. Those with a winning attitude view life as fun and are thankful for the talents and abilities that God has given them. With this kind of attitude, you can lose a football game by 100 points and still enjoy playing. You can come in fifth place in a speech contest and still have fun because of the people you met and the opportunity you had to share your thoughts. If you can remember that winning and fun are not always equals, you're going to have a winning attitude.

Remember that winning and fun are not always equals.

When you compete, do your best. God has given you talents to use to the best of your ability. Doing your best is a way of giving glory to God for what He has given you. It's important to understand that God's love is not based on what you do or how good you are at what you do. He loves you simply because you are His creation. You may be the last one picked on every team, but you are still number one with God. God won't get down on you because you lose the big game, make a mistake on your solo performance, or spend the rest of your competitive years on a losing team. He'll always pick you for His all-star team. If you can come to understand this truth, you'll be able to do your best for God and you won't have negative competitive attitudes. You will handle losing as easily as winning because you know that God has you on His team.

Something to think about:

"Everything you say and everything you do should all be done for Jesus your Lord. And in all you do, give thanks to God the Father through Jesus" (Colossians 3:17).

MY PERSONAL THOUGHTS AND ACTION STEPS:	

52
GIVE YOURSELF A BREAK

I read a newspaper article which documented major problems facing teenagers—divorced parents, alcohol, drugs, sex, abortion, and suicide. The article then stated a number of ideas for solving these problems. I was surprised that none of these ideas dealt with a teenager's development. I really believe that problems and acts of rebellion reflect the larger problem of development. For example, when I talk with Joshua about his frequent thoughts of suicide, I can see that his problems are a result of the person he has become throughout his growing years.

A deeper problem that the article writer failed to acknowledge is the issue of self-love. It's a fact that teenagers in general don't like themselves. Self-hatred among students seems to be at an epidemic level! I think the lack of self-love among students results when they compare themselves with each other and try to conform to each other.

When you compare yourself with others you will always end up feeling like a loser. That's because you will always find someone who is stronger,

> *When you compare yourself with others you will always end up feeling like a loser.*

smarter, more athletic, or better-looking than you. You aren't being fair to yourself. You may have nine positive qualities and one negative quality. But when you compare your one negative quality to someone else's positive quality, you consider yourself a failure. For example, I live in a very nice house. But when I look at the houses around the lake in our community, my house looks cheap by comparison. My house is great; it has everything we need. But the lakeside homes are so nice that I'd love to live in one of them. By comparing homes I feel guilty that I can't provide a better living environment for my family.

Another thing which destroys our self-love is conformity. As we look for acceptance among our peers, we tend to want, buy, and wear only the things which are "in." Since we desire acceptance, we want to be like those that our society has held up as popular. For example, recently I went shopping for my first pair of glasses. Since I know nothing about glasses, I asked the optician a lot of questions about different styles of frames. He proudly held up one model and said, "This is the style that everybody is buying." It seems so natural for us to want what everyone else has. We are happy to be Xerox copies of others because it's safe.

We are happy to be Xerox copies of others because it's safe.

When it comes to comparison, God uses different standards to judge us. Human standards change all the time, but God's standards have always been the same; they never change. He looks at our hearts. He doesn't care if we are tan, fat, thin, have zits, or can't make the athletic team. We can rest in the fact that throughout history God has been interested in people's hearts. That will never change.

Conformity plays no part in God's plan for us either. He

wants to *trans*form us, not *con*form us. To transform means to change in form and appearance. Change is the key word. When we change we are doing the exact opposite of conforming. Again, God is concerned about the heart. He wants our hearts changed so that our thoughts will be directed toward Him.

Something to think about:

"Do not change yourselves to be like the people of this world. But be changed within by a new way of thinking. Then you will be able to decide what God wants for you. And you will be able to know what is good and pleasing to God and what is perfect" (Romans 12:2).

MY PERSONAL THOUGHTS AND ACTION STEPS:	
	_____
	_____
	_____
	_____
	_____
_____	
_____	
_____	
_____	
_____	
_____	

53

GIVING: THE PERCENTAGE GAME

Our world is filled with takers who will receive whatever they can get their hands on. It's no secret that we live in a self-centered society which tells us to look out for number one—ourselves. Even we Christians are not free from this selfish attitude. Our churches and their ministries rely on the faithful giving of Christians. But so many believers find it difficult to give their money to benefit the mission of the church. Are you one of these Christians? Do you find it difficult to part with your money? Do you know that giving is an action step of your faith?

When we would take an offering at our youth group, we barely collected enough money to pay for the envelope in which we sent it to the office. But when the group went out for brunch after church, students shelled out all kinds of money for their food. This made me mad. But as I talked with students about their money, I began to understand that they were uneducated about giving.

> *Giving is an action step of your faith.*

In the Old Testament, people were required by law to give a portion (called a *tithe*) of their money. When all of the requirements were added up, they had to give over 20 percent of their income to God's work. In the New Testament, we find that we are no longer under the law and required to give. We are under the new covenant of Jesus which calls us to give as we prosper. Jesus got upset with the Pharisees when they were more concerned with legalistic giving than they were with showing love for God (see Matthew 23:23). Jesus is more concerned about the attitude of our hearts when we give than He is with the amount. Giving demonstrates our obedience to God. Because we love Him and have given 100 percent of ourselves to Him, we feel the need and desire to give money back to Him. Our faithful, generous giving enables ministries to continue.

> *Our challenge is to become hilarious givers.*

Since God is concerned with the attitude of our hearts, He will know if we don't want to give. The Bible says, "Each one should give, then, what he has decided in his heart to give. He should not be sad when he gives. And he should not give because he feels forced to give. God loves the person who gives happily" (2 Corinthians 9:7). Whether you give ten percent or 50 percent, the point is that you give with a cheerful heart. God will honor this and take care of you: "God can give you more blessings than you need. Then you will always have plenty of everything. You will have enough to give to every good work" (2 Corinthians 9:8). Since God honors happy givers, our challenge is to become hilarious givers.

Something to think about:

"Jesus sat near the Temple money box where people put their gifts. He watched the people put in their money. Many rich people gave large sums of money. Then a poor widow came and gave two very small copper coins. These coins were not worth even a penny. Jesus called his followers to him. He said, 'I tell you the truth. This poor widow gave only two small coins. But she really gave more than all those rich people. The rich have plenty; they gave only what they did not need. This woman is very poor. But she gave all she had. And she needed that money to help her live'" (Mark 12:41-44).

MY PERSONAL THOUGHTS AND ACTION STEPS:

_____

_____

_____

_____

_____

_____

_____

_____

_____

_____

_____

_____

54

MEASURING OUR MATURITY

The Bible is the only standard we can use to determine our spiritual maturity. We judge our maturity by the guidelines God has provided in His Word. I think it's a good practice to ask ourselves this question during a given situation: "How would a mature Christian respond right now?" In addition to considering God's Word, I like to use the following chart for mentally measuring my spiritual maturity. It helps remind me of the process that I'm involved in:

×		+
Old life	Christian life	New life

(2 Corinthians 5:17)

The × on the left represents the time when you came into a relationship with Christ. Your life before Christ is represented to the left of the ×. That period is best symbolized by the color black. The Bible refers to the old life without Christ as living in the darkness. But when you met Christ, you left the old life and entered the new: "If anyone belongs to Christ, then he is made new. The old things have gone; everything is made new!" (2 Corinthians 5:17).

> **The Bible is the only standard we can use to determine our spiritual maturity.**

The + on the right represents perfection. Its

symbolic color is white. Those who have a relationship with Christ will be seen as pure when standing before God. Until then, we are neither black nor white, but off-white, which represents the process of our faith.

When we begin our walk with God, we live on the left end of the horizontal line. This represents immaturity or being a babe in Christ. As our faith matures, we slowly move toward the right end.

It's a lifetime journey of victories and failures.

This growth is gradual, and it never allows us to reach perfection. Visualizing this movement helps us understand that Christianity is a process and not an overnight achievement. It's a lifetime journey of victories and failures.

I like to visualize my position on this scale as I continually struggle with living the Christian life. There are times when I move myself three steps toward maturity, and times when I blow it and fall two steps back. But I believe that my "net gain" of one step moves me in the right direction toward becoming a more mature man of God. My prayer is that you will be encouraged by God's grace to run the race and fight the good fight. Set your eyes on the cross and know that your maturity pleases God.

Something to think about:

"We must not become tired of doing good. We will receive our harvest of eternal life at the right time. We must not give up!" (Galatians 6:9).

MY PERSONAL THOUGHTS AND ACTION STEPS:	_____

55

LACKING A SENSE OF HUMOR IS NOTHING TO LAUGH AT

My heart breaks for people who can't find anything funny to make them laugh. There is plenty to laugh at in this crazy world. People who can't break loose and allow themselves to laugh really miss out on a great emotion.

There's not much written about laughter in the Bible. There are no verses that read, "Thou shalt laugh." We don't have any stories about Jesus cracking jokes to His disciples. Nor do we have any record of Jesus saying, "I want to teach you how to make others laugh so there will still be laughter in the world when I am gone." Just because Jesus didn't instruct us to laugh doesn't mean He didn't laugh.

Jesus is pictured in religious movies as very serious, often speaking in an intense, deep voice. He is portrayed as angelic and inhuman. But Jesus was human as well as divine, and I'm sure He laughed. Just think about the various people and situations Jesus encountered. Imagine the look on the face of the guy who was carrying the jug of water which Jesus turned into wine (see John 2). Or think about the reaction of the crowd when four guys had the guts to lower their buddy through the roof of a house where Jesus was preaching (see Mark 2). There are many events in the

> *There is plenty to laugh at in this crazy world.*

Bible that are just plain funny, especially when we consider how we would feel if they happened today.

A word used in the Bible which has a similar meaning to laughter is the word joy. There are several verses in the Bible which speak of joy and gladness. Joy in your life can bring about the needed response of laughter. Having joy in your heart makes it much easier to express and appreciate laughter.

If you have a difficult time laughing, I challenge you to begin looking for amusing situations. Many funny things happen around us every day. But often we see them as just another source of stress or as uncomfortable situations. I call these events "unmentionable commonalties." They happen all the time, but we never talk about them and rarely notice when they happen to someone else. For instance, have you ever noticed that a person who trips while walking will always look back to see what he tripped over? It's as if he's saying, "Who did that?" Or why is it that everyone takes bread from the middle of the loaf? Or what about the uncomfortable situation of your foot touching another foot under the table? You wonder how you can move your foot away so the person doesn't think you were playing footsie. These little things happen to everyone, and they can be funny if they are viewed in the right way.

A great tragedy of modern time is that many people take life far too seriously.

A great tragedy of modern time is that many people take life far too seriously. They forget to laugh. They are so concerned about building their mountain of personal credentials that they forget about the mud puddle at the bottom where they need to play occasionally to maintain their sanity. If you can learn to laugh at yourself in spite of your weaknesses, you will be able to develop a great sense of humor. Laughing is similar to crying—it's an emotional release. If you use this emotion in a positive manner, it can become a great source of happiness and overflowing joy. Keep laughing!

Something to think about:

"A happy heart is like good medicine. But a broken spirit drains your strength" (Proverbs 17:22).

MY PERSONAL THOUGHTS AND ACTION STEPS:

56

FROM OBNOXIOUS TO MEEK: IS IT AN IMPOSSIBLE CHANGE?

Why is it that obnoxious people seem to get a lot of attention? The obnoxious people I know are always looking for extra attention by trying to force themselves into the spotlight. They're usually good people, just not fun to be around.

The opposite of an obnoxious person is a meek person. I know very few people who exemplify this quality. It's difficult to obtain. Before I understood the term, I associated meekness with weakness. I thought a meek person was spineless; someone who didn't have any opinions, couldn't speak in front of others, and didn't have fun. But as I observed my meek friends and studied the life of Jesus, I discovered that I was wrong.

Jesus was both meek and influential. He spoke His message in front of thousands, exercised His power and authority to heal, raised people from the dead, and was a leader of many. On one occasion, Jesus entered the Temple in Jerusalem to find a swap meet in operation. People were selling animals for sacrifices and money changers were charging outrageous rates of interest. Jesus reacted with anger and strength, chasing the irreverent crowd out of the Temple with a whip. He

I associated meekness with weakness. I thought a meek person was spineless.

183

overturned their tables and yelled at them for making His Father's house a market (see John 2:13-16). Yet Jesus' gentleness is seen when He gathered children into His arms and blessed them (see Mark 10:13-16). He's a perfect example of a meek man.

The Bible equates meekness with humility. Nowhere in Scripture are meekness or humility seen as negative traits. The meek and the humble are mighty in God's eyes, as illustrated in the passage complimentary of Moses's character: "Now Moses was very humble. He was the least proud person on earth" (Numbers 12:3).

Someone who is humble enjoys being the behind-the-scenes person. He doesn't crave the spotlight of attention. The humble person is truly joyful when others receive attention.

A meek person is a servant. Jesus is the ultimate example of servanthood. His greatest act of servanthood was giving His life so that we might live eternally. Those who possess the quality of meekness are the greatest servants.

Meek people serve in small ways. They are the first ones to volunteer for tasks. They don't race to be first in line. They sit in the backseat of the car so others can enjoy the comfort of the front seat. They pick up the litter that you and I walk past. They bring in the neighbors' trash cans. They give up their seats so others can have them, and they wait in lines to buy tickets for their friends, while their friends play around.

A meek person is a servant. Jesus is the ultimate example of servanthood.

A meek person is gentle, displaying a quiet spirit and possessing a confident peace. Their actions are gentle and caring. I've heard the term meek used to describe a tamed stallion, a wild and powerful horse that is gentle enough to be a child's pet.

How can an obnoxious person learn the quality of meekness? An obnoxious person needs to be slow to speak. This is a tough one for me. I always want others to hear my opinion. I usually sit at the edge of my seat so that I can put my bits of wisdom into the conversation. But meek people are in control of their tongues, following James' advice: "Dear brothers, always be willing to listen and slow to speak" (James 1:19).

An obnoxious person needs to put others before himself. This may sound like a simple rule, but it's difficult to put into practice. Our meek friends are servants, able to put others before themselves. Being a servant is a response to our faith in Christ. We don't serve in order to receive rewards or admiration. We serve because we love God and are challenged to imitate Jesus' example.

We are often kept from being meek by our overinflated ideas of who we are. We think we are something, but we are nothing compared to God. David praised God for His greatness and majesty, but considered himself a worm. This is the attitude of fearing God. David wasn't afraid of God, but in awe of Him. When we understand how awesome God is, we will be able to see ourselves in better perspective. This perspective helps us put our obnoxious need for attention behind us and focus on being like Jesus.

Something to think about:

"I tell you the truth. You must change and become like little children. If you don't do this, you will never enter the kingdom of heaven. The greatest person in the kingdom of heaven is the one who makes himself humble like this child" (Matthew 18:3-4).

MY PERSONAL THOUGHTS AND ACTION STEPS:

_____

_____

_____

_____

_____

_____

_____

_____

_____

_____

_____

_____

_____

_____

_____

RUNNING ON EMPTY AT THE GAS PUMP OF LIFE

All of us want to know about the future. Where will I go to college? What will I do for a living? Whom will I marry? Some of us are desperate when it comes to wanting to know. It's a constant frustration trying to figure everything out. The irony is that we want to know God's plan for our lives, but we are unwilling to spend the time necessary to discover it. Isn't it true that one of the easiest aspects to flake off on in our faith is our time with God? We say that we love Him, we've given our lives to Him, and we trust Him to take control of our lives. But we can't seem to find time to spend with Him. And we complain because we don't know what to do with our lives.

This dilemma is like a car out of gas. The car won't move on until it is filled with gas, and we won't move on in life unless we keep our spiritual tanks full. Fortunately, we've run out of gas at a gas station. All we have to do is fill up. But instead, we just sit in the car hoping it will fill itself. And since that doesn't happen, we remain stranded.

One of the easiest aspects to flake off on in our faith is our time with God.

Many Christians are stranded. We desperately want to know the truth. We want to know God's will for our lives. We want His help in making decisions. We need His guidance for our behavior in specific situations. And we want to know more about God. But we don't take time to be with Him in order to find these answers.

God desires to reveal these answers to us. He has chosen to communicate to us in different ways. He has given every believer His Holy Spirit, who communicates to us in silence. How often do you listen to God? Do you ever take time to be quiet and allow Him to speak to you through your thoughts? It's difficult to be quiet and listen when we surround ourselves with stereos, Walkmans, and televisions. I know very few teenagers who feel comfortable with silence.

God also uses other people to communicate to us. For centuries God has used messengers to communicate His truth. Every Sunday we hear from others. This is usually the easiest form of learning, which is why many of us tend to settle for only this one form of listening to God.

God's Word, the Bible, is filled with answers to our questions and needs.

God's Word, the Bible, is filled with answers to our questions and needs. The Bible is God's playbook. It's God's way of showing us how to operate as Christians. God knew we would need help and direction for growth, and that's why He made the Bible available. Reading the Bible for ourselves is an important means of keeping our tank from running empty.

I've heard a lot of students kids complain about reading the Bible. Some say the Bible is boring because it's difficult to understand. My suggestion is to find a Bible that's easy to read. There are several different translations that might be better suited for your reading and comprehension level. The Scriptures used in this book are quoted from *The Everyday Bible: New Century Version* (Worthy Publishing). It's a translation with a third-grade reading level (I use this one because I need all the help I can get!).

Another complaint is, "I've already read it." What we fail to understand is that our perceptions continue to change. Each time we read the Bible, we get something different as a result of our changing perceptions. God may be trying to communicate a new truth to you when you read a passage you've read before.

If you want a fresh approach to your time with God, you might pick up the book *Creative Times with God*, by Doug Fields (Harvest House Publishers). It will get you more involved in the Bible through a variety of study methods.

When we count on growing through only one of these three means of communication, we run on empty. Coming to church once a week is like trying to learn football by attending a weekly coach's meeting. Football is a game that needs daily instruction and training. Depending on a once-a-week, 20-minute lecture will not adequately equip you to play a good game. And attending

Coming to church once a week is like trying to learn football by attending a weekly coach's meeting.

church is not enough to equip you for life. You also need to listen and read. You need personal instruction from God's playbook.

God wants you to have answers to your questions. He

wants you to know more about Him so that the journey of Christianity isn't a game, but a relationship with a personal and intimate God. I know it's tough to listen to God and read His Word, but this is how He has chosen to communicate with us. He's made communication available; don't allow yourself to run on empty.

Something to think about:

"All Scripture is given by God and is useful for teaching and for showing people what is wrong in their lives. It is useful for correcting faults and teaching how to live right" (2 Timothy 3:16); "Always remember what is written in the Book of the Teachings. Study it day and night. Then you will be sure to obey everything that is written there. If you do this, you will be wise and successful in everything" (Joshua 1:8); "God's word is alive and working. It is sharper than a sword sharpened on both sides. It cuts all the way into us, where the soul and the spirit are joined. It cuts to the center of our joints and our bones. And God's word judges the thoughts and feelings in our hearts" (Hebrews 4:12).

MY PERSONAL THOUGHTS AND ACTION STEPS:

58

ALLOWING GOD TO USE UNLIKELY CANDIDATES

Potential is a word you probably don't hear much about. It's a popular term in the business world. Companies try to figure how to reach the maximum potential for their advertising dollars. There are several books and seminars which try to help people reach their maximum potential. The success of a business is often determined by its ability to mobilize potential.

There seem to be two opposite patterns of thought concerning potential and Christians. One holds that Christians have no potential. When we come into a relationship with Christ, we empty ourselves of all human abilities and skills. Then we bow in submission to God and He becomes a puppeteer, moving us around according to His plan. The other extreme contends that God has already equipped us with everything we need to be successful. We don't need God; all we need to do is tap into our potential.

> *God seems to choose ordinary people to accomplish His extra-ordinary work.*

The Bible provides a balance to these views. I believe God has given us potential to do great things. It's our job to be available to God, and it's God's job to use us. Availability is what makes us successful in God's eyes. Scripture reveals that God's job description for successful servants is very different from the world's. God seems to choose ordinary people to accomplish His extraordinary work. God uses people we view as unlikely candidates.

The Book of Exodus explains how God delivered the Israelites from captivity and bondage. He chose Moses to lead the Israelites out of Egypt. Moses had escaped Egypt earlier as a murderer. He didn't even want the job of being Israel's leader. He had no desire to be used by God. But God had different plans. He used an unlikely candidate to get His job done. Powerful leadership skills don't seem to be a major element on God's job description for success.

Then there's the story of David and Goliath, and the war between the Philistines and the Israelites. Goliath was a huge professional soldier, an animal. He was stronger than several men. But

> *Make yourself available and God will use you.*

David was a young, inexperienced kid whose job was to take out the trash and feed the sheep. God used him to plant a pebble in Goliath's face and knock him out. Age and abilities don't seem to be in God's job description either.

There's the apostle Paul who, previous to his encounter with Christ, burned churches and arrested and stoned Christians. And yet when God captured Paul's heart, He used him to start churches and write half of the New Testament. A questionable past doesn't seem to deter God from using someone.

When you look at God's job description for successful people, you may think He's going to require leadership skills that you don't have. You may think that your age will hurt you, or that God will question your abilities. At the very least, you probably think you will be disqualified because of your faults and sins. But after looking at the examples of Moses, David, and Paul, you must realize that all God wants you to do is write your name next to these as an unlikely, but available, candidate.

If you are going to allow God to work through you as an unlikely candidate, you can't wait for all your problems to get solved or for all the obstacles to be removed. If you do, you'll be waiting forever. Don't spend your entire life preparing and planning to be used by God instead of being used. Make yourself available and God will use you.

Something to think about:

"Since God has shown us great mercy, I beg you to offer your lives as a living sacrifice to him. Your offering must be only for God and pleasing to him. This is the spiritual way for you to worship" (Romans 12:1).

MY PERSONAL THOUGHTS AND ACTION STEPS:	_____

_____
_____
_____
_____
_____
_____
_____
_____
_____
_____
_____

59

CAN I DO ALL THINGS?

I want to end this book by looking at the meaning of Philippians 4:13, a great passage: "I can do all things through Christ who gives me strength." By now you realize that this journey called the Christian life is an ongoing process, not an overnight transformation. And during the process of growing as Christians, we have God's written promise that we can do all the things He wants us to do through the strength of Christ. My hope is that you will be encouraged to attempt great things in your life now that you know that Christ's strength will help you accomplish them.

I have broken the verse into several small sections. I want to explain each section and give you an action step for each one.

I can: *Can* is a simple word which is future-oriented. The action step for this word is *expand your vision*. You already know that God uses unlikely candidates like you and me to do His work. So expand your vision to think what God can do through you in the days, months, and years ahead. Be future-oriented. Think about what can happen if you open yourself to God's plan. Dream.

> **Christian life is an ongoing process, not an overnight transformation.**

Explore. You'll find that God is much bigger than you presently think. With whom do you want to share Jesus this year? What do you want to accomplish? What aspect of your lifestyle do you want to change? What new skill do you want to learn? You'll be amazed at what God's strength can do through you.

Do: This is an action word. It involves movement. The action step for this word is *exercise your gifts*. God has given you incredible gifts. Don't just sit on them or hide them behind excuses. You'll never know the potential of your gifts unless you exercise them.

All things: There is no limit to what we can accomplish with God's strength. But we often limit God in our lives by thinking there are things He can't do. The action step here is *explode your stereotypes of God*. Each one of us has our own ideas of what God is like and what He can do. We put God in a box, and when we need Him to do something that we think He can do, we take off the lid and allow

> *You'll never know the potential of your gifts unless you exercise them.*

God to do His work. By thinking this way we not only put God in a box, but we limit what He can do through us. We put *ourselves* in a box: a preconceived prison of what we think we can and can't do. I can't imagine how many good works have been left undone by those of us who have limited God's power.

Joe, a Jewish boy, had been attending our church for several months, but had openly said he would never become a Christian. One day I overheard a member of our youth group confronting Joe: "Why do you even come to church? You've said for the last nine months that you will never become a Christian. Why are you here?"

His words made me angry. Later I pulled him aside and said, "Our God is bigger than your ideas of what He can do. He's even more powerful than what Joe said about never becoming a Christian." This truth became a reality when Joe accepted Christ at our summer camp.

Through Christ: This is how we are able to do all things. This is the backbone of the verse. It isn't through ourselves that we do all things, but through Christ. The action step here is *experiment with obedience*. What does it mean to be obedient to Christ? The Bible is filled with great men and women who were heroes of the faith because of their obedience, not their talents. In what areas of your life and problems do you need to increase your obedience?

Who gives me strength: Strength comes from God when we allow Him to work. The action step for this phrase is *expect God to work*. God is not in the business of letting us down. He's not a cosmic killjoy who gets His kicks, like we do, when others fail. He promises to be there and to strengthen us. Expect that to happen.

Notice that two of the most important words in the verse are also the smallest: *I* and *me. I* and *me* point to you. You must be willing to admit your problems and your powerlessness to solve them without God's help. It's at this point when you'll be able to expand, exercise, explode, experiment, and expect. God will keep His strength coming, but you must turn it on and use it.

Something to think about:

"I know how to live when I am poor. And I know how to live when I have plenty. I have learned the secret of being happy at any time in everything that happens. I have learned to be happy when I have enough to eat and when I do not have enough to eat. I have learned to be happy when I have all that I need and when I do not have the things I need. I can do all things through Christ because he gives me strength" (Philippians 4:12-13).

MY PERSONAL THOUGHTS AND ACTION STEPS:

_____

_____

_____

_____

_____

_____

_____

_____

_____

_____

_____

_____

_____

_____

_____

Other Good Harvest House Reading

GETTING IN TOUCH WITH GOD
by *Jim Burns*

This daily devotional will take you to Scripture and provide practical application in such areas as love, prayer, the Holy Spirit, and the promises of God.

RADICAL RESPECT
by *Jim Burns*

In a society permeated by sex and permissiveness, straight answers to questions about sexuality are still hard to come by. In *Radical Respect,* noted youth pastor Jim Burns balances straightforward discussion of real-life situations with God's original plan for sexuality.

BIBLE FUN
by *Bob Phillips*

From bestselling "clean joke" humorist Bob Phillips, author of over 20 books with more than 2 million copies in print, comes *Bible Fun.* Jam-packed full of brain-teasing crossword puzzles, intricate mazes, word jumbles, and other mind benders, *Bible Fun* will keep you occupied for hours—with the added bonus of honing up your Bible knowledge. Sharpen your pencil and put your thinking cap on—you're about to be a-maze-d!

GOD'S DESIGN FOR CHRISTIAN DATING
by *Greg Laurie*

In the midst of conflicting worldly standards, it is still possible to find and fulfill God's design for exciting relationships with the opposite sex. Offering godly counsel with touches of humor, Greg gives the "how-to" of healthy dating.

THE ULTIMATE BIBLE TRIVIA CHALLENGE
Combined edition of *In Search of Bible Trivia I and II*
by *Bob Phillips*

Test your Bible knowledge to the limit with this ultimate collection of Scripture facts. Over 1700 trivia questions makes sure that, whether you're a new believer or an old saint, you'll find hundreds of questions just for you—from easy quizzes to advanced brain-teasers. You'll find dozens of ways to use Bible trivia questions— with friends, on family game nights, or break into teams for competitions similar to "college bowl" or "Jeopardy."

Dear Reader:

We would appreciate hearing from you regarding this Harvest House nonfiction book. It will enable us to continue to give you the best in Christian publishing.

1. What most influenced you to purchase *If Life is a Piece of Cake—Why Am I Still Hungry?*
   - ☐ Author
   - ☐ Subject matter
   - ☐ Backcover copy
   - ☐ Recommendations
   - ☐ Cover/Title
   - ☐ _____

2. Where did you purchase this book?
   - ☐ Christian bookstore
   - ☐ General bookstore
   - ☐ Department store
   - ☐ Grocery store
   - ☐ Other

3. Your overall rating of this book:
   - ☐ Excellent ☐ Very good ☐ Good ☐ Fair ☐ Poor

4. How likely would you be to purchase other books by this author?
   - ☐ Very likely
   - ☐ Somewhat likely
   - ☐ Not very likely
   - ☐ Not at all

5. What types of books most interest you?
   (check all that apply)
   - ☐ Women's Books
   - ☐ Marriage Books
   - ☐ Current Issues
   - ☐ Self Help/Psychology
   - ☐ Bible Studies
   - ☐ Fiction
   - ☐ Biographies
   - ☐ Children's Books
   - ☐ Youth Books
   - ☐ Other _____

6. Please check the box next to your age group.
   - ☐ Under 18
   - ☐ 18-24
   - ☐ 25-34
   - ☐ 35-44
   - ☐ 45-54
   - ☐ 55 and over

Mail to: Editorial Director, Harvest House Publishers, Inc.
1075 Arrowsmith, Eugene, OR 97402

Name _____

Address _____

City _____ State _____ Zip _____

Thank you for helping us to help you in future publications!